When the Monkeys Run the Zoo

Stefan Kühl is professor of sociology at the University of Bielefeld in Germany and works as consultant for Metaplan, a consulting firm based in Princeton, Hamburg, Shanghai, Singapore, Versailles and Zurich. He studied sociology and history at the University of Bielefeld (Germany), Johns Hopkins University in Baltimore (USA), Université Paris-X-Nanterre (France) and the University of Oxford (UK).

Other Books by Stefan Kühl:

Organizations. A Systems Approach
(Routledge 2013)
Ordinary Organizations: Why Normal Men Carried Out the Holocaust
(Polity Press 2016)
Sisyphus in Management: The Futile Search for the Optimal Organizational Structure
(forthcoming)
The Rainmaker Effect: Contradictions of the Learning Organization
(forthcoming)

To contact us:

Metaplan
101 Wall Street
Princeton, NJ 08540
USA
Phone: +1 609-688-9171
stefankuehl@metaplan.com
www.metaplan.com

Stefan Kühl

WHEN THE MONKEYS RUN THE ZOO

THE PITFALLS OF FLAT HIERARCHIES

Organizational Dialogue Press
Princeton, Hamburg, Shanghai, Singapore, Versailles, Zurich

ISBN (Print) 978-0-9991479-0-0
ISBN (EPUB) 978-0-9991479-1-7

Copyright © 2017 by Organizational Dialogue Press, Princeton, Hamburg, Shanghai, Singapore, Versailles, Zurich

Translated by: Lee Holt
Cover Design: Guido Klütsch
Cover Motif: istockphoto.com/4x6
Typesetting: Thomas Auer
Project Management: Tabea Koepp
www.organizationaldialoguepress.com

Contents

On Trumpets, Pyramids, and Onions—Foreword

It all began with a trumpet, a pyramid, and an onion. The idea for this book came to me while I was looking at a sketch by an organizational consulting firm that illustrated the development of economic organizations since the beginning of the nineteenth century. The drawing presented the deeply subdivided, narrow hierarchy of organizations around 1900 in the shape of a trumpet. Organizations were defined by a clear structure with unambiguous lines of command. The organization's leader alone had an overview and issued instructions accordingly. Command and obedience were the pillars of organization.

As companies and administration became more complex and middle management began to expand, the trumpet became a pyramid. Increasing numbers of people were assigned responsibility for planning, management, and review duties. Functional subdivisions were formed, and the competences and responsibilities of discrete departments were delimited from one another. Two new elements expanded the repertoire of organizational tools: staffs to support upper management, and matrix management as a kind of transverse hierarchy. Increasing levels of automation and computerization led to a further expansion of management, despite a shrinking foundation.

Organizations reacted to the rapid transformation of markets and other technological upheavals with workshops that brought together employees from different functional roles. Project groups increasingly supplemented conventional hierarchies. Pyramid-shaped organizations began to resemble an onion. However, the "onion shape" was not the last metaphor that would serve to represent the organization of collective action. New "post-onion" organizational concepts arrived on the scene at an ever-faster pace, with names such as the "learning company," the "agile organization," the "modular firm," the "fractal factory," or the "cellular system."

In this book I examine how managers, consultants, and scholars conceive of organizational structure in a post-onion age. As an organizational scholar, I am not in a position to promote new forms of organization as a panacea for a crisis in bureaucratic organization that has already existed for quite some time. In defiance of the general enthusiasm for new organizational concepts that come to the fore again and again, this book examines the difficulties, weaknesses, and limits of post-bureaucratic forms of organization. I look at the past experiences of companies, administrative bodies, and political organizations with the breakdown of their hierarchies and efforts at decentralization. I argue that the drive to break down all boundaries, both internal and external, threatens to "diffuse" the entire organization, to deprive organizations of their internal cohesion. Employees lose a clear image of their organization (the identity dilemma). Organizations dedicated to innovation and change create zones of insecurity within their organization that threaten to foster a "permanent politicization" of internal processes and decision-making (the politicization dilemma). Ever more organizations are resorting to streamlining strategies in reaction to increasing complexity, yet it is precisely this impulse toward the simplification of processes that leads to growing complexity, even if it is not perceived as such (the complexity dilemma).

Beyond the Dramatization of Innovation

Readers who are looking for the latest management methods to spruce up their upcoming PowerPoint presentation or to bring a new consulting service to the market will not be happy with this book. In most cases, the presentation of over-hyped innovative organizational concepts is really just a repackaging of the post-bureaucratic organizational principles that have been known quantities for some time. There were experiments quite early on in Germany and the United Kingdom with partially autonomous production groups, an idea that has been presented each decade as a revolutionary discovery under some new name. The demand to break down hierarchies in organizations found expression in the work of the pioneering management thinker Mary Parker Follett (1941: 158), who for decades called for the replacement of "vertical authority" in organizations by a "horizontal authority."

Innovation in new post-bureaucratic organizational concepts has come to rest almost exclusively on the invention of new terminology. Yesterday's "flexible firm" is today's "agile company" and probably tomorrow's "systemic operation." The "adhocracy" of yesterday is today's "team-based organization," and perhaps tomorrow it will morph into a "holacratic organization." Much-vaunted "expert networks" are marketed today as "communities of practice" and will probably become "crowds of wisdom" tomorrow. If we gain some distance and perspective, however, this urge to dramatize innovation is understandable. Managers entering a new organization often feel compelled to expound on conceptual innovations to show that they will approach things differently than their predecessors. Consultants find themselves competing with other consultants not just for clients, but also for claims to authority over organizational concepts, leading them to invent new buzz words over and over to impress their clients. Financial journalists can hardly sell their readers—who are oriented to current developments— the idea that, despite all of the imagination that goes into inventing new management concepts, everything often still remains in principle the same in organizations. This is why the financial press is always there to cover developments when a new idea is trotted out.

However, the invention of ever-new terms for post-bureaucratic forms of organization cannot conceal the fact that the problems largely remain the same. In my critical examination of ostensibly new organizational principles, I therefore refer to the verbal excitement in management literature merely to present fundamental scholarly insights into the ways in which post-bureaucratic organizations function, and to do so in such a way that will facilitate discussion among practitioners. It is not my objective, however, to include an analysis of the most recent shift in management discourse; I assume that this book will put readers in a position to identify the central organizational principles in the latest iteration of management concepts, and to build a bridge to the problem areas of post-bureaucratic organizations as described here. Whoever knows what troubles face "adhocracies" or "team-based organizations" will also recognize the basic problems of similarly constructed "agile," "holicratic", "modular," "fractal," or "cellular" organizations.

The Three Sides of Organization

If we want to understand organizations, we have to distinguish between three relevant aspects:[1] The *formal side* of organizations deals with the written rules and official requirements that the organization's members—at least in their presentation to other members—must observe or fulfill if they want to remain members of the organization. An *informal side* always emerges as well because only part of the expectations within organizations can be regulated via the formal side. We are dealing here not just with thinking patterns and forms of perception that are typical to organizations; instead, this is about expectations of action that are not aligned with the organization's formal requirements, or may perhaps even contradict them. An organization presents itself to the outside world with its *display side*. The display side of an organization can contain elements of its formal side, which is particularly the case for administrations and hospitals, but this side consists to a significant degree of general value formulations that enable the organization to appear attractive in its environment; however, because these value statements are so abstract, they can only serve as general orientation points for organization members, if at all.

The narrow focus of literature about new forms of organization is frequently due to the fact that, in many cases, scholars comprehend organizations primarily from their display side. This literature is presented as though the success stories repeated ad nauseam by management gurus—which find their way into PowerPoint presentations shown at conferences by managers from pioneering organizations, or the zealously proclaimed success recipes from consultants—are supposed to represent the reality of organizations. The implication here is that the formal structures (meaning the factual hierarchical relationships and programs of work) and informal structures (which means routines that have crept in) are identical to the structures presented on the display side.[2]

But if we take a closer look at the management literature from long-vaunted pioneering organizations—firms such as Semco, W.L. Gore & Associates, Mettler-Toledo, Enron, Apple, Spotify, or Morning Star—it rapidly becomes clear that the management bestsellers from consultants, the Harvard Business Review, or PowerPoint presentations only present the display side of these pioneering organizations.[3] Often, if we pose just three or four questions about formal communication paths, we discover that an organization with 5,000 employees that presents itself as a learning organization due to its flat hierarchy doesn't have just the officially announced five levels of hierarchy; there are actually fourteen. And sometimes we need only ask for the personnel statistics to find out that a fluctuation rate of 40 percent per year cannot support the reported levels of employee satisfaction.

It would be wrong, however, to discriminate against representations of the display side of companies, administrations, hospitals, armies, or political parties as just elaborately constructed Potemkin villages. It may sound persuasive whenever, for example, Robert G. Eccles and Nitin Nohria (1992: 1) proclaim that, "words come and go," but "actions will remain the central maxim of management." However, they fail to recognize that the production of "words"—especially of "beautiful words"—is an important task for management. Visible sides serve an important function for organizations: they produce legitimacy, help to soften the impact of contradictory requirements, and reduce internal conflicts because they obviate the need to carry out every conflict in public. This is what makes attempts at professional display side management quite understandable. Every manager or consultant who publicly extols a company or administration as a decentralized flat-hierarchy organization is worth the money, as long as their claims are not preposterous. However, we would be making a fundamental error if we were to mistake these prettified representations for the reality of organizations.

In this book, I apply a perhaps unusual methodological device. I take the managers and consultants from leading organizations at their word and show what would happen if companies, administrations, hospitals, and universities actually functioned in the ways that they represent through their display side. Even if we were to use organizational science to think through the principles presented on the display side—to think them through to their logical end—it is clear that pioneering organizations would have significant problems in the formation of a uniform identity, that power struggles would increase rather than decrease, and that complexity within the organization would explode.

The Contradictory Nature of Organizations— On the Relationship of Theory and Practice

Originally I had conceived of this book as a kind of early warning system for organizations that wanted to embark upon the adventure of replacing their strongly hierarchical, bureaucratic forms of organization with de-hierarchalized, decentralized ones. This book should serve as an admonition, a warning about new kinds of coordination problems that organizations sign up for if they abandon the time-tested division of labor based on hierarchy and functions. In view of the massive difficulties that arise in reorganization processes meant to dismantle hierarchies and implement decentralization, this book however serves the purpose of offering an explanation to those organizations who run into fundamental problems when introducing decentralized structures. It offers patterns of explanation that do not attribute difficulties to the failure of any one individual, but rather to needs for coordination for which we do not have a handy solution.

I wrote this book from the very specific perspective of systems theory. At the moment, this is perhaps the most theoretically ambitious and most interesting approach in organizational science. It is based on the assumption that an organization's expectations—just like the expectations of other social entities, such as small families, groups of friends, or protest movements—are always contradictory, and that organizations themselves must, to a certain degree, be contradictory themselves in order to be able to meet the requirements of their respective environments.[4]

These contradictions, however, are systematically concealed in conventional management literature. Even if the harmonious image of organizations is not always presented in the heavy-handed manner of manuals with titles that promise practitioners how they can make their organizations simultaneously "more humane" and "more productive" (cf. Meltzer/Nord 1981), the management literature nevertheless offers a glimmer of the promise that the contradictions inherent in every organization can be reduced towards zero.

Systems theory, however, takes a look at the differences between various departments and teams, between different levels of hierarchy, and between the display, formal, and informal sides. The rationalities, ways of thinking, and perspectives that necessarily result from the division of labor in organizations can be worked out in a systematic way such that we do not lose touch with the "whole entirety" of an organization.

If we systematically work out the problems of specific organizational principles and present them to practitioners in companies, administrations, armies, hospitals, political parties, or associations, we always hear the same question: how we are supposed to deal with this? Often this question betrays a hope for a quick fix, for a rapid solution for the problem. As an organizational studies scholar, I could take the easy road and refer to the fact that scholars—at least those who take themselves seriously as scientists and do not abuse their university positions to market their own organizational concepts—are merely responsible for analyzing organizations.

I don't intend to avoid this question completely, though. At the end of the book, I present relevant search strategies that organizations can use to strike a balance between stability and change. I show that the management literature assumes that the self-organization of decentralized units can only thrive in a condition of unlimited instability, which is a state in which neither inflexibility nor explosive chaos has the upper hand. This kind of management locates "stabilization concepts" of post-bureaucratic organizations, such as exercising influence by specifying contexts or techniques, beyond the realm of order and chaos. These concepts appear to be a first response—even if it is an unsatisfactory one—to the dilemmas of identity, politicization, and complexity.

1.
Monkeys, Revolutions, and Post-bureaucratic Organizations

We don't want to stare into the window of the future.
She's lying with the past in bed.
The first men were not the last monkeys
And where there is a head, there's often a board.
Erich Kästner

"I won't have the monkeys running the zoo." Such was the response of Frank Borman, the former CEO of the U.S. company Eastern Airlines, to a demand by company employees for stronger involvement in decision-making processes within the company (cf. Peters 1988b: 343). In the same way that this statement—in its purpose and contemptuous equivalence between employees and monkeys—is an expression of traditional thinking in certain management circles, the vehement rejection of such statements by new, and sometimes not so new, management gurus testifies to a new kind of thinking about how organizations should be structured in the future. The American management consultant Tom Peters and his "in" colleagues use these kinds of quotes to set their organizational concepts apart from traditional management thinking. If things were to go their way, the organization of the future would be a hierarchy-free, democratic, highly innovative, and flexible economic organization in which the prosperity and welfare of workers is subordinate only to the well-being of customers.[5]

For managers in Europe, America, and Asia who are regularly unsettled by crises, such proposals always fall upon open ears. Many labor unions, however, are not sure whether they should view new management thinking as simply more sophisticated strategies of control, or whether they can really count on a true humanization of working life. Examples from the USA and Europe show that ideas for a fundamental redesign of the organization of economic activity are successful, both in the form of bestselling books as well as actual practitioners; major service companies are trying to find a way out of the hierarchy trap with quite profound decentralization. Production companies are hoping to gain a competitive advantage by introducing semi-autonomous production teams. And administrations, hospitals, universities, and schools are increasingly taking on the tenets of "new public management," which consists of decentralization concepts that were first tried out in the private sector.

However, those reports about restructuring in major organizations that reach the public via management magazines and the financial pages of newspapers are merely the tip of the iceberg. It is becoming clear that there is a need for a major shift in the ways in which organizations are organized. Self-proclaimed management gurus, organizational consultants, and some organizational studies scholars do not hesitate to speak and write about the "necessity of a revolution" (Peters 1988a; 1988b: 3ff.), a "true revolution" (Crozier 1989: 21; Millot/Roulleau 1991: 12), or even a "cultural revolution" (Landier 1991). The "Handbook for Revolutionaries" (Tichy 1993) was directed at managers. As different as the specifics of their observations, ideas, and recommendations for the future may be, they all agree on one thing: the time of upheavals, of the "gentle revolution," has begun. A zoo managed by the monkeys is on the horizon.

Reports from decentralized organizations, however, suggest that the "gentle revolution" may be anything but gentle. As soon as a concept pertaining to decentralization or leveling hierarchies, complete with a catchy name, has established itself in the financial papers and in management, we begin to hear the initial press reports about how the reorganization measures have failed. At first glance, it is with an astonishing regularity that management concepts are pushed through in companies, administrations, hospitals, universities, or schools, only to disappear after a certain time due to reports about failed attempts at restructuring. Typically a new revolutionary concept is rung in with a management bestseller full of promises for major gains in productivity, revenue, and profits, with examples of successful organizations and recipes for do-it-yourself change management. The consulting companies follow in short order, standing ready to help managers who didn't manage to attain the efficiency improvements promised by the do-it-yourself method. After two or three years, the first doubts begin to surface. Scientific-sounding surveys are presented, claiming that only 20 to 30 percent of all streamlining, re-engineering, or chaos management projects are successful.[6] Financial publications that had fully participated in the general celebration of the discovery of an ostensible "philosopher's stone" now report intensively on failed attempts at restructuring.

The explanations offered for the failure of these restructuring attempts typically refer to resistance, deficiencies, misconduct, and misfortunes among the personnel involved; the failed streamlining of organizations is attributed to strong contradictions within middle management, a lack of team work among employees, a lack of expertise on "lean" reorganization among the managers responsible for its implementation, and a "lack of acceptance" caused by too little information and participation. The collapse of "re-engineering projects" or "agile software projects" is explained as the selection of the wrong plan, the missing connection between the project and the organization's strategy, insufficient presence in the management team, and a lack of knowledge about the "how" of implementation.[7]

Overall, the short-term effusions for a management concept are countered by a surprising deficit of convincing explanatory models for the problematic developments that are currently underway. Many management consultants and scholars may create breathtaking proposals for organizations, yet their analyses of potential difficulties suffer from pronounced shortsightedness. Without further ado, many consultants place the blame for problems in the restructuring process on inappropriate staff, averting their eyes from the structural problems that issue from decentralization. They then place their trust in solutions based on new, fashionable concepts, or rely on a mix of East Asian religious mysticism, pseudo-rational motivational theories, psychosocially oriented esoterica, and their own "intuition."

But the academic disciplines of business studies, occupational psychology, and industrial sociology all come up quite short as well in their analyses of new forms of organization. Although these disciplines are able to describe production concepts such as Lean Production, Material Requirement Planning, Just-in-time production, and semi-autonomous manufacturing groups, their analyses of problems rarely address the roots of measures meant to increase flexibility. Problems are all too quickly attributed either to poor interface management or successful employee resistance against subtler forms of control by management. Frequently, business studies, occupational psychology, and industrial sociology do not have a comprehensive framework for classifying new organizational concepts. One expression of this lack of theoretical constructs is the exponential increase in "posts" in the terminology of business studies and occupational sociology: the "post-bureaucratic organization" (Heydebrand 1989; Heckscher 1993; Alvesson/Thompson 2005) is understood as the result of a shift towards "post-industrialism" (Bell 1973), "post-Fordism," (Lipietz 1993; Gee/Hull/Lanshear 1996), to "post-economism" (Palloix/Zarifian 1989), or even to "post-capitalism" (Drucker 1992).

Conscious of a certain terminological speechlessness, I use the term 'post-bureaucratic organization' in order to examine to what extent and by what means "new" forms of organization should be distinguished from "old" ones, and why new problems tend to arise. The summary of various attempts at decentralization carried out under the moniker of the post-bureaucratic organization should facilitate answers to the question of whether the introduction of new types of organizations is really a "true revolution"—a process of fundamental and profound changes—or a "revolution from above," a "pseudo-revolution" in which the only thing at stake is management adjusting its language to new requirements. These observations respond to the question of why major problems come up when introducing new organizational concepts.

The word "revolution" describes an abrupt break with the past, the breakthrough of a new existential order, and it implies an overthrow of power relationships. Such conditions would surely exist if—as certain organization representatives and management consultants claim—

new organizations were oriented towards complete flexibility and an absolute capacity for transformation, and if their employees were the "new powers that be." A shift to this kind of organization—in our society, shaped as it is by bureaucratization, hierarchalization, and the division of labor—would certainly earn the name of an organizational revolution. This book inquires whether such a form of organization exists, and, furthermore, whether it can exist at all.

The management literature's proclivity for laying claim to the term "revolution" enables me to sort through, expose the problems of, and scrutinize the materials used: Against what forms of organization do post-bureaucratic organizations define themselves? To what long-familiar organizational principles do they refer, and what is new about them? Why does the propagation of new forms of organizing collective action predominate in discourse about management? Are the assumptions presented on the organization's display side—change as the only stable thing, and employees as new potentates—convincing? How can organizations oriented towards innovation and flexibility hold together? To what degree do relationships to other organizations, customers, and suppliers change?

In the first chapter, I take my analysis of these materials one step further, showing that current management literature suggests—unjustifiably so—that it offers convincing, consistent concepts for post-bureaucratic organizations. More often, post-bureaucratic organizations face three basic problems: securing the identity of change-oriented organizations, regulating non-transparent power structures, and dealing with internal complexity.

In the second chapter, I show that organizations are confronted with the problem of having to decide between establishing routines and opening up to organizational change. In Taylorist bureaucratic thinking, organizations strived to attain the best possible routines: stability and redundancy were the watchwords. Because of new technological possibilities and profound changes, however, there are now new kinds of demands for flexibility and innovation in organizations. Organizations have to find methods and ways to turn these external uncertainties into new internal measures that can move them forward.

Innovation, flexibility, and the capacity for change are becoming basic conditions for successful economic activity.

In chapter three, I present the developments that would have to hold true in the management literature for a "true revolution" to take place in economic organizations. Flexibility is the maxim towards which new forms of organization are oriented. The formation of profit centers and market networks are leading to the development of a new kind of more intensive relationships between organizations and the environment. The strict division between market and hierarchy as opposing principles in the organization of collective commercial activity is dissolving. The internal organization, the "guts" of post-bureaucratic organizations, is oriented towards the axiom of an absolute ability to change. Structures are only very loosely connected, and hierarchies are being dismantled and decentralization continues. Differentiation into departments is disintegrating. New organization structures, if they can be described at all as something fixed, require an intensification of informal, non-formalized communication. Project groups, semi-autonomous manufacturing groups, and their networks secure both the production and innovation process.

In chapter four, the core chapter of the book, I expound the problems of this development. I show that a "true revolution" would lead to the dissolution of organization over the long term. Organizations would founder on an excess of internal uncertainty. They face the basic dilemma of having to stabilize themselves, even though flexibility is important for their survival. This "identity dilemma" becomes apparent at the employee level as a "politicization dilemma": when an organization commits to innovation and change, it creates new zones of insecurity and thereby opens up new power resources for employees. Hierarchy and the distribution of skills in departments are no longer available as regulatory mechanisms for power struggles. Power relationships are no longer retained within clear structures of authority, and what results is a constant process of negotiation that leads to a "permanent politicization" of internal processes and decision-making. Condemned to become ever more complex, post-bureaucratic organizations resort to efforts at simplification that seem as though they might reduce complexity. These simplification processes, however, lead to an increase in complexity in everyday practices. The "complexity dilemma"—the futile attempt to reduce complexity by means of simplification—drives organizations to the edge of manageability. Employees see themselves as exposed to demands of an entirely new dimension.

In chapter five, I speculate about possible lines of development in post-bureaucratic organizations. There are signs that organizations strive to reduce and increase complexity and insecurity. Such a process would combine two inherently opposing principles—stability and flexibility—at a higher level. Only those organizations that find themselves beyond stability and explosive chaos—so the thinking goes—can manifest a capacity for self-organization. Confronted by such complex processes of self-organization, specific answers to the worries and hardships of post-bureaucratic organizations definitely no longer feel as simple as management books and organizational consultants would often like to have us believe.

2.
The Limits of Bureaucratic-hierarchical Organizations

The Central Office knows it all. The Central Office understands the big picture, believes in the big picture, and has a map room. At the Central Office, men work together in a constant funk, but they pat you on the shoulder, saying, "My dear friend, you're in no position to judge from your individual post! But here in the Central Office ..." The Central Office's first and foremost concern is to remain the Central Office. God have mercy on the subordinate branch that dares to do something independently! Whether it's rational or not, necessary or not, or on fire or not—the Central Office must be consulted first. Otherwise, why would it be the Central Office?

Kurt Tucholsky

An important element of the criticisms levied against centralized, hierarchical organizations is the image of a divided society, a semi-democracy. Although broad parts of society are "de-hierarchalized," organizations in the economy, science, and politics are still typically democracy-free because of their hierarchical structure. Although societal fragmentation may have diminished at the overall level of society, with people developing from "subjects" to "responsible citizens," and the growing "freedom of information" in the press and television, along with global mobility, making the world "a village," similar developments have not yet taken place in organizations. Employees are still described and treated as subordinates. Basic constitutional rights, such as the freedom of expression, the freedom of speech, and the freedom to choose one's workplace, would not work within organizations. Departments would feud with one another like competitors. Today's world of organizations may still be described as fragmenting, with a dearth of coordination and a lack of freedom.

"Enlightened" management in America, Europe, and increasingly in Asia seems to be unanimous in its denunciation of Taylorism's deconstruction of work, which reduces employees to cogs in a sophisticated production machine. As early as the 1990s, the American management guru Tom Peters (1993: 198) called for the dismantling, deconstruction, and dismemberment of hierarchies. Best-selling German author Jochen Schmidt (1993: 22) announced the "death knell" for hierarchies in the form of Lean Management, cost and profit center structures, and project management. And our consulting colleague Eike Gebhardt (1991: 133) has described hierarchies as an "obsolete model." The advocates of bureaucratic, hierarchical forms of organization may have had the upper hand in organizational practice, but they lost the "battle" waged in management journals and in organizational leadership seminars by the early twenty-first century.

In a time in which terms such as hierarchy, centralization, and Taylorist optimization have become dirty words among managers, we have to recall that bureaucratic or Taylorist-Fordist organization represented a significant improvement over the conventional forms of production prevalent at the beginning of industrialization. The routinization of work processes, the breakdown of production sequences, and the structuring of organizations according to "Scientific Management" (Taylor) guaranteed a stability that created the foundation for the mass production of goods to satisfy the basic needs and consumer needs of broad swaths of the population (at least in Western states). This chapter shows that there is a general trend in organizations to establish routines to meet their need for certainty (Section 2.1). In the practice of bureaucracy and Taylorism, the establishment of redundancies was elevated to an all-powerful maxim. The forms of organization that resulted were extremely stable and perfectly suited to an environment that only changed at a very slow pace (Section 2.2). Rapid market changes, the globalization of markets, and technological upheavals led however to demands for flexibility and innovation to which the conventional forms of organization were not capable of responding (Section 2.3).

2.1 Organizations and their Preference for Certainty

Formal structure: this is what makes organizations different from the diffuse, arbitrary interaction among friends, in waiting lines, or at the bar. Organizations need formal communication processes and formal programs so that they can become an organization at all. They cannot offer the pleasant informality and irregularity found among friends or at the bar. It is only because organizations have a formal structure that one can become a member at all. Without structure, there is no membership—and we could add that without membership, there are no organizations. This is because organizations need clear ideas about who belongs to them so that they can develop structures. The wild carousing of students only becomes a fraternity if a group of men come together, draft a charter, apply to a national organization for authorization to found a local chapter, and then begin pooling their funds for the collective purpose of throwing some legendary parties. Not everyone can be part of these select circles. The organized increase of alcohol consumption remains the preserve of a clearly defined group. Rules and membership are mutually dependent on one another.

The "privilege" of membership in a fraternity, in a political party, a company, a sewing club, or perhaps in some famous rabbit breeders' association, requires that members recognize and obey certain membership rules. Otherwise, the top leaders in a company would be the people who can do the most beautiful needlework, who can open a beer bottle with their teeth, or who can breed the largest dwarf rabbit. Compliance with membership rules is guaranteed by the structure of offices, resource distribution, responsibilities, command hierarchy, control mechanisms, and communication paths. At first, it doesn't matter whether we are talking about an international media corporation, the social welfare office around the corner, or a small animal breeders' association.

The provisioning of membership and non-membership through the distribution of party books, signing an employment contract, or simple non-written agreement may be the fundamental condition for the existence of an organization, but it does not suffice to fill that organization with life. An organization first comes into being through decision-making (Luhmann 2000: 123ff.). Decisions are their elixir of life. They transform various possibilities into something unambiguous. Decisions condense many possible futures into one unique reality.

An organization gains greater stability by means of connecting organizational boundaries, decisions, norms and identities than through spontaneous interactions. This is why many sewing clubs, fraternities, and companies last longer than the waiting line at the box office or the relaxing walk that ends at the corner bar. Organizations embody, on one hand, the limitation of possible actions and the discipline of spontaneous and relatively disorderly communication processes; on the other hand, they also offer stability and certainty, which opens up new opportunities. Organizations are therefore simultaneously more and less than groups of friends, waiting lines, or unstructured drinking bouts.

Always the Same, or Different

Every manager and every employee is familiar with this phenomenon: the central problem in organizations is the coordination of collective action. If it weren't necessary to have to constantly agree on collective action, then a lot of things would be much easier, and many everyday conflicts would not come up. People do not have the same freedom in organizations that they have among their friends; in the latter group, you should be able to talk about everything, do anything, and try anything out, at least theoretically. Organizations do not exist for the pure joy of being together. They have a purpose.

So how can we coordinate collective action towards fulfilling this purpose? Roughly speaking, there are two options, which admittedly may sound rather banal: either you make decisions like you always have, meaning that you repeat an action, or you do something new. Systems theory refers to these two options as redundancy and variance. Redundancy—which means repetition and/or stability—is the structural restriction of decision-making contexts (Atlan 1979). Redundancy is at its highest if a single piece of information is sufficient to recognize an entire organization (cf. Luhmann 2003) and to predict its behavior. Variance—or, somewhat more vaguely, change or flexibility—describes the diversity of decisions. The organization's behavior, and behavior within it, is changing constantly.

All organizations—our international media corporation as well as our rabbit breeders' association—face the challenge of finding a reasonable balance between stability and flexibility. They have to strive to find a middle way between the "self-induced paralysis of perfect order" (dictatorship) and the "arbitrariness of perfect disorder" (anarchy) (Willke 1989a: 96f.). Niklas Luhmann describes the paradox that an organization needs stability and flexibility, yet cannot aim for both at the same time. Organizations generate stability by means of hierarchy and thereby produce the necessary order for production processes. At the same time, however, companies are subject to the laws of change because of competitive conditions. Change and stability seem to be an opposing pair of concepts because change leads to a disruption in the established order. On one hand, organizations strive for flexibility to adjust to a changing environment, and on the other hand they have an internal yearning for stability (cf. Thompson 1967: 10ff.). Stability is the prerequisite for technological efficiency, economization, predictability, and controllability. Flexibility is required to guarantee organizational adaptation, effectiveness, and a capacity for dealing with unpredictability.

A Soft Spot for Security and Certainty

Every dismissal and every new hire, every innovation and every investment, every vendor change, every bribe and every development of a new customer base, can be reduced in the final analysis to one point: how does an organization deal with internal or external uncertainty? Uncertainty describes the extent to which change or flexibility is allowed within an organization. Organizations—and in this way they are not all that different from many people—appear to have a predilection for reducing this uncertainty: new employees bring along a bit of unwelcome commotion at first; we prefer suppliers and customers whose payment and delivery patterns we already know, and we most prefer to deal with a problem in a time-tested way. There is a tendency, which is fully understandable, towards a one-sided focus on certainty to create assuredness and to minimize risk (cf. Thompson 1967: 152). The conservative election slogan of "no experimentation" draws upon this deeply embedded inclination. If you are not in the middle of a full-blown crisis, then you stick with tradition, which is often—at least in our own perception—what we know works. Luhmann identifies a permanent proclivity to condense structures and thereby increase stability (2003). Loosely speaking, this means the following for organizations: despite all of the hype about innovation and flexibility, the normal mortal manager still has the secret dream that every work process can be costed out and standardized ad infinitum, which would lead to staff behavior becoming fully quantifiable and controllable. Only a chronic workaholic would find the perfectly designed, seamlessly functioning organization to be a horror film. The only problem for the manager is that, because this idealistic utopia renders "management" itself superfluous, this organizational dream would become a nightmare from the purely personal perspective of the manager.[8]

The fact that organizations have a soft spot for certainty and stability can be explained by the fact that organizations, because of the history of their genesis and differentiation, are geared towards the conservation of structure, and have to be. They define themselves against the anarchy of absolute freedom precisely through the narrowing of the range of opportunities and reducing the number of events that could occur. Business strategies therefore understandably aim at organizing the technical and social structures required to reach an organization's goals in such a way that the company avoids conditions that create uncertainties within the organization.

2.2 Taylorism and Bureaucracy:
The Victory of Eternal Repetition

In the conventional bureaucratic, hierarchical, Taylorist and Fordist form of organization, this penchant for certainty is not just taken into account; the generation of stability was declared to be the cure-all for the successful and efficient management of organizations.[9] The dream of a controllable and simultaneously highly efficient organization seemed to have become a reality after the end of the nineteenth century, in the course of the second industrial revolution. Orienting an entire organization towards stability was supposed to make the behavior of workers, departments, and customers more predictable in general.[10]

At the beginning of the twentieth century, Frederick Winslow Taylor, an American engineer and founder of Scientific Management, described the separation of planning and controlling functions from the executing functions as a basic condition for effective organization. According to his ideas, every detail in the production process had to be analyzed and scientifically understood. The next step was to take production activities, which were broken down to the smallest level and required minimal skills from workers, and reassemble them in organizational terms. People and machines would be geared together like a clockwork mechanism (Taylor 1967; see also Braverman 1974: 112-121). His organizational principle could be summed up into an easy formula: "Previously, personality stood first and foremost; in the future, the organization and the system will take its place." The principle developed by Taylor was applied consistently by Henry Ford, the founder of the Ford Company and the driving force behind the introduction of mass production in the USA. He integrated Taylor's principles in his automobile factories and extended them beyond the actual production process. In Fordism, the entire spectrum of business activity—from the acquisition of raw materials to the sale of finished goods—was subjected to a process of rationalization oriented towards the principle of Scientific Management.

At the same time as Taylor was establishing the principles of Scientific Management, the German sociologist Max Weber was developing his theory of bureaucracy, which had a trajectory similar to that of Taylor's thought. Bureaucracies are defined by fixed official rules. The activities necessary to sustain a bureaucracy are clearly distributed and distinctly defined. Supervisors with the power to make decisions coordinate the various fields of activity. Written documents guarantee control of and compliance with instructions (Weber 1976: 551ff.). Although Weber's theory of bureaucracy was developed in the context of public administration, it can often be applied to private companies, labor unions, and political organizations. Despite all of the popular demonization of bureaucratic tendencies in modern societies and the widespread rejection of the "depersonalization" typical of bureaucracy's "administration of things," we should not forget that it is precisely the predictability of bureaucratic processes—even if it is the ability to anticipate that nothing will move and nothing will happen—that enabled such an enormous evolutionary leap: the precision, consistency, discipline, strictness, and reliability of bureaucratic action gave the rulers and the ruled the certainty to perfect their achievements (cf. Perrow 2007: 24ff.).

Eberhard Schnelle points out the similarity of bureaucracy and Taylorism: "the administrative work, the making of decisions, the work of monitoring, controlling, and planning were schematized according to the same methods and simplified, as we know from the processing of materials in a factory: labor was divided." The resulting multi-unit forms of organizations, Schnelle noted, could only be held together and coordinated by one method: hierarchy. And "hierarchy ensured stability and continuity" (Schnelle 1989: 1). The bureaucratic assurance of mastery in organizations and the increase in organizational efficiency seemed to be inextricably linked and mutually reinforcing.

These three components, which are so fundamental to Weber's theory of bureaucracy and Taylor's Scientific Management—unbundling, standardization, and the formalization of processes—offered the certainty upon which states were able to conduct their (sometimes bureaucratic) escapades in parliamentary democratic rule and the consumption-oriented distribution of mass products. These two developments are closer to one another than we may sense at first glance.

Both Taylor and Weber were confident that their models guaranteed the highest degree of speed, objectivity, and efficiency. In terms of technical performance, no other form of organization would be capable of taking up rational bureaucracy or scientific management (cf. Weber 1976: 578f.). Taylor's "one best way" for an organization, and Weber's "rationality" of bureaucratic activity, show that they invest a basic trust in an organization to consistently apply their principles and to align and set them up in a stable and efficient way.

Formalization: the Remedy for Uncertainty

In Taylor's and Weber's thought, the consistent formalization of all intra- and inter-organizational processes was meant to reduce uncertainty to near zero. Formalization is a term that describes a social process in which a "series of operations is artificially fixed and made repeatable, predictable, and executable for others" (Rammert 1988: 162), and with which organization members can be compelled to comply with rules under the implicit or explicit threat of termination (Luhmann 1964: 29ff.). Complete certainty through the full programming of activities would then be attained if every relevant event were to become a stimulus for a clearly defined reaction. It was justly said of the French telephone company France Telecom that a small cough by Chief Executive Marcel Roulet in the morning would automatically lead to the entire company having runny noses by noon. Minimal information is enough to set in motion entire organizational processes. If it were possible to completely establish and fix the behavior of all parts of an organization, and in response to changes in the market, then this would result in a company like the one that the former head of ITT, Harold Geneen, wanted: even Mickey Mouse could run it.

Everything is clear in formalized, hierarchically coordinated organizations. A nearly absolute predictability prevails. Such organizations are organized "perfectly" by means of regulations and expectations: guidelines govern everything and everyone exactly, "so that no one causes or adjusts anything" (Fuchs 1993: 26). The roles of managers and employees within this kind of structure are simple, clear, and relatively constant. The boundaries within the organization function like labels on a map. They make it very clear who reports to whom and who is responsible for what, thereby directing and coordinating the behavior of the individual and making it useful for the entire organization (Hirschhorn/Gilmore 1992).

Formalization occurs through the determination of "decision-making premises" (Simon 1957) for members, meaning decisions that apply for more than just one decision (cf. Luhmann 2003)—and in a Taylorist or bureaucratic ideal, to everyone. Bureaucracies aspire to formalization by pursuing clearly fixed distributions of activities, rigid departmental boundaries, precise workplace descriptions, inflexible organization of authority, and regimented processing procedures. The Taylorist principle is a scientization of management. Knowledge about undocumented work processes is supposed to be wormed out of employees and transformed into rules, formulas, and laws formulated with the help of scientific methods (see Braverman 1974: 112ff.; Zarifian 1990: 13ff.).[11]

What do these formalization media look like in particular? Organizations can establish decision-making programs in the form of rules, guidelines, or laws. These can be programs that aim at a specific result. They can also include conditional programs that, in the case of a defined input, restrict the latitude for decisions or, in an ideal case, make decisions. The second instrument for increasing stability focuses on determining *communication paths*. The prime example is hierarchies with their regimented, channeled information flows. Organizations, however, can also guarantee stability through *people*. A person's skill and predictability enables us to predict how they will behave in a specific situation. In this way, people are a ready-made package of decision-making premises (Luhmann 2003). These three paths to the generation of stability can be combined in the form of a position. Each position is a specific combination of programmatic, communication-shaping, and personal decision-making premises. Traditional bureaucratic organization is nowhere better characterized than in positions: descriptions of positions, advertisements for open positions, and the filling of positions.

One sophisticated way to produce stability is to use technology or machines to automate organizational processes, or even to automate entire production processes. A person cannot match the performance and reliability of a machine and therefore poses a potential factor of uncertainty.[12] A person is removed from the directly affected organizational process or eliminated by means of termination. Mechanization arranges a series of conditional programs in such a way that there are only the options of acceptance or rejection. A cigarette dispenser with an age checking mechanism, for example, can only tell the difference between "absolute identity" (cigarettes are exchanged for money) and "absolute difference" (cigarettes are not dispensed) (Schimank 1986: 81). In this kind of process, uncertainty is reduced to zero because machines can only create pre-defined connections between inputs and outputs. The use of technology to generate stability is therefore, in its deeper logic, not all that far from producing stability by means of rules, guidelines, and laws. Organizations that are hierarchical, Taylorist, and bureaucratic are also described, with good reason, as "machine bureaucracies" that view their employees as beings with limited rationality, similar to machines, that must be managed, controlled, and motivated from outside (cf. Mintzberg/McHugh 1985: 160).

What Do We Do With "Residual Uncertainty"?

The absolute removal of uncertainty remained a dream that could not come true, even for the most Taylorist of the Taylorist-Fordist companies: the Ford factories in the USA. Henry Ford once said that any of his customers could have a car painted in any color they wanted, so long as it was black. Customers only accept this as long as they don't know about a red Cadillac, a pink Chevrolet, or a blue Mercedes as alternatives. Even companies that elevated the generation of stability to a central tenet of their organization had to allow a minimum of flexibility as competition came on the scene. The Ford factories also began to bring their vehicles to the market in different colors in the 1930s, especially because of the growing competition from General Motors.

Production however was meant to continue functioning as if the market would accept a product that was always and forever the same, and as if the input into the production circuit were always of the same quality. The assumption of absolutely controllable causality allowed the productive core (typically manufacturing) to be organized according to the stability or redundancy principle, while the removal of uncertainties was delegated to fields of managerial function (cf. also Crozier/ Friedberg 1977: 165). This buffer strategy brings discernible stability for the productive core, yet it has to be gained at the expense of the organization by means of functional differentiation of departments that "process uncertainty," otherwise called "buffering units" (cf. Thompson 1967: 21). Such "uncertainty absorbers" are the upper management, the division for work preparation, the organization department, procurement and sales, and research and development. As Wolfgang Schnelle demonstrates, this principle of Taylorist organizations is mirrored in demands placed on employees. Employees are asked to show a capacity for repetition more than for change: "They should complete the tasks assigned to them in a reliable, safe, assiduous, and yet intensive way. Delight in experimentation, the ability to adapt, and a readiness to take risks are expected only from a few employees on innovative staffs" (Schnelle 1978: 1).

The Taylorist-Fordist and bureaucratic-hierarchical organizational model was broadly accepted as the most efficient form of organization. Even several labor unions came to terms with this kind of organization of collective activity as the ostensibly most rational and systematic method (cf. Linhart 1991: 26). They dealt with management questions regarding the organization of labor as second-rank, and only seemed to understand themselves as a functionally differentiated department for asserting higher wage demands.

Despite its ability within a certain framework to absorb uncertainty, the bureaucratic type of organization depends on a relatively stable environment, and this is the only point in which the contingency theory of organizational science remains valid. This stable environment was a given in the age of "mass production of undifferentiated products" (Coriat 1991: 21). Due to the homogeneity of products and a constantly growing demand, a minimum of adaptive ability was required in organizations. When a radical change in these environmental conditions changed, however, organizations had to begin looking for a new mode of organization.

2.3 Why Things Can't Go On Like This—Reasons for a Fundamental Organizational Transformation

To illustrate the limits of hierarchical, bureaucratic organizations faced with new environmental conditions, Jürgen Fuchs (1992: 17), referring to East Frisian everyday researcher Otto Waalkes (1984), describes the following fictional (!) situation in his company:

"You meet a drunk on the street. Your eye sees how the man raises his fist. In today's typical corporate organization, something like the following would happen. Your eye would send a fax to the Executive Board responsible, apologizing for the disruption while pointing out the danger and uniqueness of the situation:

Eye to Executive Board:
1. A fist is coming at us!
2. Ask the lid to close.
3. Recommend stepping aside and running for it if necessary.

Executive Board to Eye:
I don't want to create precedence. Please submit an investment application for closing the lid, including a cost-benefit analysis. As you know, I am not responsible for Point 3. Please submit a proposal to the Executive Board. I will then present your concern to the entire Board.

Eye to Executive Board:
Re: 1. The fist is getting closer and closer!
Re: 2. The cost for closing the eyelid is approximately 1.7 calories. The benefit cannot be quantified.

Re: 3. I need at least two days to prepare a proposal. I fear that it will
then be too late. I strongly recommend doing something.

Executive Board to Eye:
What does closer and closer mean? Please provide exact information!
Due to the limited investment, I could approve it if the expense is
covered by the budget. The entire Board meets next week on Tuesday.
I will expect your proposal by then.

Eye to Executive Board:
I withdraw my applications. Please call an ambulance."

Why did this method of dealing with drunks in particular and turbulent conditions in general fail after hundreds of years of success?
Fuchs identifies the reasons in the fact that, "in the rapid innovation cycles, dynamism, and globalization of markets, and with our
accelerated transformation into an information and services society,"
hierarchical and Taylorist organizational principles are pushed to their
limits (1992: 15). We find a similar smorgasbord of reasons for the
end of the bureaucratic organizational model in Tom Peters. From his
viewpoint, the high price of oil, one trillion dollars of debt in under-
developed countries, corporate mergers, disintegration, joint ventures,
technological revolutions in design, production, and distribution, new
international and domestic competitors, and changing tastes lead to
the necessity of organizing organizations in a fundamentally different
way (Peters 1988b: 36f.).

   We have to conduct a closer analysis of the interaction of these
causes if we are to avoid following Fuchs and Peters into an all-too-
global explanation for the transformation from a bureaucratic Taylorist
model to new, decentralized, and de-bureaucratized forms of organization. There are two rough lines of explanation. One approach is based
on the assumption of a fundamental change in market demand, and
the other on a technological revolution unleashed by the development
of information and communication technologies. Both interpretations
are often sequenced in the form of a list, or one approach is derived

deductively from the other. In the following, I attempt to establish the relationship between these two approaches and to unite their effects on organizations by focusing on demands for innovation within companies.

Market and Technology

The crisis in the mass production system led to mass unemployment in the 1970s and 1980s, sagging growth in the industrialized countries of the West, and dramatically shrinking industrial sectors (cf. Piore/Sabel 1984). An aggressive price war took place in the remaining markets for mass products. An essential reason for this critical situation was the tendency towards saturation in markets for mass products; in this sense, the mass production model produced its own crisis. It bumped up against its inner limits. It triumphed to death.

Demand shifted more and more towards highly differentiated products; people wanted their own "personal" car, one that completely corresponded to their own demands and that was as different from other vehicles as possible. Companies had to expand their product portfolios, increase the number of versions on offer, shorten product cycles, and submit to special individual requests. The relationship between quantity and quality was reversed. While production activity formerly aimed at putting out the greatest possible volume, now the emphasis shifted to quality, combined with comprehensive service.

This interpretation of the crisis relies on the "market pull theory," which views the technical and organizational transformation as based in changing demands. It bears similarities to classical economic theory, which presumes the primacy of needs. In the strict market economy version of this theory, technology—and in a certain way organization as well—is a material that is shaped only by the selective forces of calculating cost and benefit. This approach stands in opposition to the "technology push theory." In its extreme version, this theory assumes that technology determines social and organizational developments.

Contrary to multiple fears, the introduction of information and communication technology did not lead to the total control or marginalization of employees, nor the elimination of their jobs. Instead, it seems that information and communication technologies—taking organizational changes for granted—have increased the options available to organizations. The view of the businessman Gerard Endenburg was probably characteristic for him and his colleagues when he said that information technology was a revolutionary development that affects all areas of daily life; he claimed that this revolution improved the ability to master organizations and to make secretiveness an increasingly expensive and useless undertaking (Endenburg 1986: 4).

Yet how do these observations fit together with the Taylorist strategy outlined above, of using technology to create stability and reduce uncertainty? In order to dissolve these seemingly opposed tendencies, let us take a closer look at the structure of information and communications technology. These new kinds of technology deal primarily not with material products but instead with systems of symbols, the connection of signs. These technologies are therefore only secondarily used to mechanize cycles that were still at the forefront in the phase of industrial technologization.

The ability to unite and flexibly combine components of a business process at a symbolic level—whether as images, texts, or workpieces—facilitated the coordination of departments that previously worked in isolation from one another, unlike machines, which only focus on specific operations, information and communication technologies focus on overall business processes. The systematic character of information and communication technology only comes into its own, for example, if we connect CNC-controlled processing machines used in production with order processing.

The systematic character and flexibility of information and communication technologies create the conditions for more effective, more adaptable production, for saving costs through cost-effective machine capacity utilization, for reducing storage costs, and for accelerated materials flow through networks at the intra- and inter-company level. At the same time, however, this process makes it impossible for a company to continue protecting its productive core against outside influences. Information and communication technologies introduce the uncertainties of demand fluctuations directly into the production process. Managerial function areas, such as work preparation or procurement and sales, lose their role as a buffer and thereby their claim to existence. The separated execution of standard processes and flexibility requirements is no longer a given. The time that remained in a Taylorist-Fordist company to slowly introduce innovations into the production process no longer exists under the conditions of new information and communication technologies. These technologies enable, and require, decisions without delay.

Information and communication technologies blow away the traditional stability-inducing effect of technologies, as we can still see in machine systems. At first glance, information and communication technologies should generate stability. They set up decision-making premises and structured lines of communication. Ambiguity is transformed into clarity. Formal rules, bureaucratic procedures, and external controls can be integrated into computer software (cf. Heydebrand 1989: 341). Nevertheless, information and communication technologies go hand in hand with an "inherent complexity" due to their integrating and networking character. Information networks become vast and unmanageable, beyond individual control because of their complexity. Information and communications technology, deployed for the purpose of reducing complexity, actually undermines its own objective. Ulrike Berger (1988: 116) compares this process to the race between the tortoise and the hare: You've just increased computer capacity in order to reduce complexity in the organization by introducing formalizations, and then elevated complexity and uncertainty are "already there," creating new additional information needs. These new information needs supply the occasion to engage in new rounds of increasing computer capacity in an ostensible attempt to reduce complexity. It is precisely the "internalization" of formal rationalities, predictabilities, and procedures that enables and requires the development of coordination mechanisms at a higher level. This leads to an increasing need for communication in highly technologized organizations.

Interactions Between New Technologies
and Changing Market Conditions

We have seen, from the viewpoint oriented towards the changing market as well as from a technology-centered perspective, that we must expect stability-producing mechanisms to fail and a rise in uncertainties. The consequence is that we have to be prepared for an explosive increase in the need for coordination within a company. The addition of two tendencies that both aim in the same direction does not suffice, however, to explain the extraordinary dynamism to which organizations are currently exposed. This is more about a development in which technological transformation and changes in demand mutually reinforce one another; to put it differently, to be stuck in a dynamic feedback imbalance. To understand this assumption, we have to resolve—in the sense of the Hegelian dialectic—the artificially constructed opposition between "market pull theory" and "technology push theory," which means to maintain the peculiarities of both theories while dissolving the dichotomy in order to combine them at a higher level. Technological developments are always responsive to possible market gaps or oriented to potential weaknesses in existing systems. A technical invention can change the interpretive framework of economic subjects in the market, thereby assuming a central position in economic contexts of interpretation and extending itself into a comprehensive technical development. Technologies often bear a need-shaping function within themselves.

A free interpretation of the concept of technological convergence (Rosenberg 1963) allows us to find an explanatory approach for the instability of environmental conditions that currently confront business activity. Technological convergence describes a universality of technical procedure that make it possible to transfer this technology from one area of application to another, almost without any problems. Information and communication technologies satisfy this condition of universality to a much stronger degree than the tool machines that initially inspired the development of the theory of technological convergence. Thanks to their universality, information and communication technologies bear the temptation of nearly limitless application. Potential customers are unable to resist this lure, or only with great difficulty. The increase in demand leads on one hand to the further expansion of the universality of information and communication technologies, and on the other to an opportunity to prove their potential in specific fields of application. In this process, production techniques (in this case, information and communication technologies) and product diversification (expressed in rising demand for "diversity") escalates in a constant imbalance.

Innovation: The Implementation of Environmental Complexity in Internal Complexity

Rapid economic, technological, environmental, and social developments increase complexity for organizations and are experienced there as uncertainty. The complexity of an organization's environment is related to the variety and mutability of the framework conditions in which business activity must take place (cf. Lawrence/Lorsch 1967: 6). The stronger and more dynamic the competitors, the more hotly contested the markets, and the more broadly distributed and demanding the customers, then the greater the complexity of an organization's external environment will be. The more technological alternatives that are available in a value creation process, the more unpredictable employee behavior is, the higher the investment volumes, the shorter the product cycles, the more complex the internal environment.

Organizations must (or at least had to) react to an increasingly turbulent environment by increasing their own options to take action. As we know from contingency theory (Burns/Stalker 1966), configuration theory (Mintzberg 1979), and systems theory (Luhmann 2000), organizations react to complex environmental conditions by increasing their own complexity. Organizational or technological innovation aims to break out of routines; products are supposed to be manufactured and sold in a more cost-effective and effective way, or completely new kinds of products are supposed to be developed. The emphasis on a company's own innovation ability seems to be the cause for the success of post-bureaucratic organizations, at least according to the financial press. Management consultants from Tom Peters (1988b: 333ff.) to Peter F. Drucker (1992: 97) promote innovation ability as a central dogma for successful organizations or those that want to be.

The reason seems simple: increased complexity in the environment of an organization necessarily leads to that organization becoming more innovative and capable of change. These increased possibilities for the organization are perceived by their external environment—for example, by other organizations, environmental protection initiatives, political institutions, or customers—as an increase in their own environmental complexity. The external environment can only respond to an organization's increased capacity for change by means of increasing its own freedom in decision-making and its own options for action. The organization in turn perceives this as an additional increase in the complexity of its environment; what from the external environment looks like decision-making freedom (contingency) means uncertainty (complexity) from an organizational viewpoint (Luhmann 1984: 249f.). The dynamic of modern society arises from this insoluble imbalance between contingency and complexity. Because of this instability in capitalist societies, it is not enough for organizations to work towards ideals described in management cookbooks or seemingly ideal organizational conditions. Instead, the internal organization must be designed in such a way that constant change is possible.

3.
Change Above All Else—The New Revolutionary Organizations

The paradigm change
I sit by the roadside.
The driver changes the wheel.
I do not like the place I come from.
I do not like the place I am going to.
Why with impatience do I
Watch him changing the wheel?
Bertolt Brecht

It stands to reason that the enthusiasm of post-bureaucratic organizations for the slogan, "Change is the only constant," which is part of an organizational vision that is impossible to fulfill, or perhaps even a neo-capitalist fantasy, must be dismissed. In every organization that champions itself as a pioneer for innovative organization structures, we see results that suggest that things cannot have gone so far with innovative organization structures (see Tomaney 1994: 157ff.). But is it an indisputable fact that management, their consultants, and frequently employees as well, believe in the postulate of total change, and that this leads to changes in organizations that are perceived as radical. The consensus is that we not only have to do away with the old forms of hierarchical organization, but that we also can dispense with them thanks to more promising alternatives.

The new forms of revolutionary organization, if they actually exist, have a history. There is already significant empirical research about organizations that have to work under turbulent, highly complex conditions, whether the study by Burns and Stalker (1966) about electronics firms, by Lawrence and Lorsch (1967) about a company in the plastics industry, the case studies of Chandler and Sayles (1971) about NASA, of Galbraith (1973) on Boeing aircraft, and of Mintzberg and McHugh (1985) about the National Film Board of Canada. Different models with adventurous names have developed, based partly on this empirical research and partly on theoretical acrobatics: "adhocracies" (Toffler 1971; Mintzberg 1979; 1988), "integrative-innovative systems" (Kanter 1983), "synthetic organizations" (Thompson 1967), "organic forms of a company" (Burns/Stalker 1966), "temporary society" (Bennis 1966), "Theory Z" (Ouchi 1981), "Model J" (Aoki 1988), "System 5" (Likert/Araki 1986), "multicellular organization" (Landier 1989), "modular factory" (Wildemann 1994), "fractal company" (Warnecke 1993), "intelligent organization" (Landier 1991), "learning organization" (Senge 1990), the "flex-firm" (Toffler 1990), the "teal organization" (Laloux 2014), the "agile organization" (Holbeche 2015) and—one of the earlier high points of this nomenclature—the "holocratic organization" (Robertson 2015).

We can learn by observing flexibility-oriented forms of organization of "revolutionary elements" that also exist in traditional organizations. Departments that were responsible for the production of flexibility in bureaucratic-hierarchical organizations (cf. Thompson 1967: 11) have structures similar to those of post-bureaucratic organizations. Furthermore, companies in highly innovative industries, such as mechanical engineering or software development, are increasingly forced to migrate to one of the new forms of organizing collective economic activity. This is why the following chapters frequently confront the more or less current "buzz words" in management literature: Just-in-time production, Lean Production, agile product development, organizational culture, post-modern factory, team work and partially autonomous work groups, adhocracy and holacracy, modular organizations and cellular systems.

In this chapter, I take post-bureaucratic organizations and their management gurus at their work and show how organizations that prescribe complete flexibility can be organized. After pointing out the new kinds of organizational relationships to the environment (Section 3.1), I discuss the inner structure of post-bureaucratic organizations, which are oriented towards loose connections (Section 3.2). I then conclude by substantiating the "organization of flexibility" by means of describing team work, project organization, and network structures (Section 3.3). In this chapter, I situate the discussion in management circles within a theoretical framework in order to make clear the connections of different aspects of post-bureaucratic forms of organization. As empirical material, I use the often euphoric presentations of post-bureaucratic organizations by managers and management consultants. If we take the most unbelievable claims made by management and their consultants seriously, this enables us to understand how a "revolution" in the organization of collective activity looks, or would look, in their imagination.

3.1 New Relations Between Environment and Organization

"Our dream (…) is a limitless company, (…) in which we rip down the walls that separate us, both internally from one another, and externally from our most important reference groups" (see Hirschhorn/Gilmore 1992). This is how the former head of General Electric, Jack Welch, described his company's aim. His statement sums up the thrust of post-bureaucratic organizations: it is about limitlessness, within and without. Just as internal organizational boundaries and blockades must be broken down, post-bureaucratic organizations want to do away with the boundaries between internal and external reference groups (customers, suppliers, competitors, interest groups).

In the moment in which an organization's environment is constantly changing, familiar and ritualized organization-environment relations lose significance and can even be dangerous for the organization. Mercedes-Benz's firm belief that customers would buy their "weapon-free assault tanks" (as a Green politician once described the S Class) on the basis of the Mercedes emblem on the hood is disastrous whenever both product diversification and product development are exposed to strong dynamism. In Taylorist-Fordist organizations, the problem of changes in the environment or the markets was assigned to "work environment experts." The procurement and sales departments, and marketing, represented the contact point between organizations and their environments. Their task was to provide a buffer against the uncertainties of the outside world, and if uncertainty could not be avoided, then careful organizational changes could be made by means of circuitous management decisions. The prevailing dream, which sometimes became reality, was that the environment could be controlled with the penetration of standardized mass products. It was possible under such conditions to firmly align departments with a contact function to the organization by means of decision templates and fixed communication paths.

The more uncertain the environment situation became, however, the more necessary it was to grant these contacts greater autonomy in dealing with environment relations. In extreme cases, some areas that were meticulously shielded from the outside world were called upon to take up relations with the environment: the assembly line worker of a major U.S. automobile manufacturer who personally drove to car buyer to repair a production error that he himself had caused was celebrated widely in the U.S. media. The fact that at the high point of shipyards crises, production employees from Endenburg Elektrotechniek were going to customers themselves to get sales orders would be sanctioned in many traditional companies as the inexcusable violation of a taboo.

We can frequently observe developments in companies that, in other types of organizations such as administrations, hospitals, universities, or schools, are often carried through only after a few years' delay. In Lean Management, for example, the intensification of relationships between production and suppliers was elevated to a central dogma. Interlacing end assembly and suppliers into an integrated organization group was supposed to facilitate a vibrant exchange between skilled workers. This in turn was meant to guarantee a decentralized, coordinated removal of errors and intense training on new machines. Because of the pioneering role of companies for other types of organizations, it is worth taking a closer look at the changes in this organization typology.

The Market and the Organization as Two Extreme Forms of Coordinated Economic Activity

In order to understand the new dimension of relationships between the environment and the organization, there have been several attempts to destroy the "myth" that the market and the organization are two fundamentally different things. Both transaction-cost economics (cf. Williamson 1975; see also Williamson 1980) and action-oriented organizational sociology (Friedberg 1992) scrutinize the artificial dichotomy between the market and the organization. Both are viewed, in their ideal form, as two extremes on a continuum of possibilities for institutional coordination. On one hand, there is complete market economic organization, in which every market participant is an owner of the means of production, so that no one is subjected to monitoring and instructions from third parties, making each participant fully responsible for their own success or failure. The "invisible hand" of the market guarantees the coordination of individual needs and interests with society's existing requirements (Smith 1937). The institution of short-term purchasing and services contract law corresponds to this concept as an ideal model. These contractual relationships, which are fully communication through the market, exhibit high flexibility and low stability. They are extremely flexible, fungible, and innovative, yet have a limited long-term orientation and little resilience or coherence. At the other extreme we have complete hierarchy, in which the abilities of participating organization members are merged in such a way that success can only be attributed to an individual in a limited way. The U.S. economic historian Alfred D. Chandler (1977) wrote that, during industrialization in the USA and Europe, it was hierarchical forms of organization, not market mechanisms, that governed the coordination of economic activity and the distribution of resources: Adam Smith's "invisible hand" of the market was replaced by the "visible hand" of hierarchical organization.

It would be wrong though to assume that collective activity is organized purely in accordance with one model or the other. Regulation performed solely by the "visible" or "invisible hand" does not exist. In a few cases we find institutionalized forms that blend market and organization. Even in the failed system of "state socialism," the ideal type of hierarchically organized regulation, we can see implicit, and sometimes explicit, coordination through market mechanisms. And the ideal type of market economy, which is often erroneously described as "deregulated" and broadly failed under Ronald Reagan and Margaret Thatcher, was controlled hierarchically to a significant degree. Under the cover of pure market economy, there formed large companies with internal and often external mechanisms of control that were structured in a hierarchical way. The "visible hand" often shakes hands with the "invisible hand" to jointly structure economic activity. Both organizational modes can become blurred in such a way that economic theoreticians Harrison White and Robert Eccles even call the market and the company as a "social myth" (1986: 136).

The hybrid forms that manage to succeed depend on environmental conditions that differ historically. In the relatively stable context of companies in the heyday of industrialized, standardized mass production, it was primarily institutionalized mechanisms of coordination that emerged, which tended very strongly towards a market-like or hierarchical structure. In a turbulent, unstable environment, collective activity is organized neither through the pure price principle, nor exclusively through a centralist company form. In this situation, post-bureaucratic companies tend to structure their market relationships more strongly through organization-specific mechanisms of coordination and to infuse their organizational structure with market mechanisms. The motto here is "networking" (cf. Thorelli 1986; Bush/Frohman 1991). Firms move in a complex environment in which we cannot imagine a company that would exist without knowledge of its relationships to other companies. Competition is more likely to take the form of positioning a company within a network, rather than penetrating markets with aggressive strategies. Developing and maintaining inter-organizational relations therefore becomes one of management's most important responsibilities (cf. Jarillo 1988).

Profit Centers and Market Networks

The tendency towards replacing strict regulation in the form of organization or the market by new kinds of intra-organizational patterns of relations is on display above all in two new kinds of institutional forms: the market network and the profit center. As the sociologist Wolf Heydebrand (1989: 346) emphasizes, they are the expression of "organic," "flexibly responsive" and "reflexive" strategies that organizations deploy against their turbulent external environment.

Profit centers are relatively autonomous departments within a company. They are performance centers that bring together activities, accountability, and competences on their own responsibility. Performance centers could be such units as pre-assembly, a paint shop, production islands, service centers, branch offices, or data processing, bookkeeping, or human resources. These different performance centers then give rise to a combined system that replaces the conventional, functionally dismembered organization.

The development towards profit and performance centers is directly connected with explosively increasing product diversification. A company that encounters a homogenous, uniform market will find it difficult to create autonomous departments (cf. Mintzberg 1979: 393). In a heterogeneous market situation, however, profit centers enable the central determination of a roughly defined product spectrum while simultaneously establishing units that are closely aligned to the market. On one hand, this reduces the risk of failure on the market—the flailing profit center is simply discarded—and on the other hand, it enables flexible and local responses to market changes. Teubner, who described the connection of profit centers as organizational networks, sees three fundamental strategies that companies use to increase their internal organizational flexibility. First, indirect context-driven control of autonomous sub-units replaces forms of direct hierarchical regulation. Rough framework guidelines are established by means of abstractly formulated company policy, indirect profit management, and management personnel policy. Second, markets within the organization replace complex chains of hierarchy in an arrangement in which relations between the profit centers and the top of the company resemble a capital market. This gives rise to internal company markets for labor, managers, resources, and products. Third, differentiation of the entire company into discrete functional units is abandoned in favor of a segmented, product-oriented scheme. While the establishment of profit centers is a strategy to increase international organizational flexibility, market networks are an entrepreneurial attempt to organize an uncertain environment and to structure it in a more fixed way. To put it differently, this is about integrating organizational elements that increase stability in turbulent, unstable environmental relationships (cf. Teubner 1992: 202).

The network approach developed by Swedish economists assumes that networks develop their strengths whenever high resource utilization and risks would override normal contractual market relations. So, for example, the (formerly existing) readiness of German companies to start their own chip production would not develop through market mechanisms alone. Instead, a network-type organization of various collective actors is needed far more. In this way, networks in unstable environmental conditions are superior for both inter-company relations organized in market terms as well as purely hierarchical forms of coordination (cf. Johannisson 1987; Johanson/Mattsson 1987).

This is why rationalization efforts at companies have been increasing taking aim at the inter-company level for a few decades. The use of new information and communication technologies enables the reorganization and better coordination of the inter-company division of labor. It becomes possible, with the aid of information technology, to couple external processes in technological and organizational terms directly to internal workflows. In this process, networks frequently emerge that are significantly more than just pure market relations.

Networks tend to have their own character. In business, networks were originally used primarily as a means to facilitate access to new markets, or they consisted of hierarchically organized relations between large companies and their suppliers (e.g., just-in-time production in the automobile industry). Increasingly, however, these forms of cooperation relate to multiple segments of the value creation chain, for example to production, procurement, and research and development. We can also see that other types of organizations—such as administrations, hospitals, armies, universities, and clubs—which in a few cases were already connected in networks at a time when this concept was scarcely known in the corporate world, are also increasingly engaging in systematic attempts to establish formalized networks.

3.2 The Guts of Post-bureaucratic Organizations

One beloved metaphor in post-bureaucratic organizations is the jazz band. The mission statement of one pioneering company in the field of decentralization claims that, "in jazz music, the integration of creative implementations is important." "Every musician"—just like every employee in the company—is said to be a "soloist who interprets a piece of music from his or her individual perspective." "The harmony of the band"—or perhaps the company—is based "on the musician's ability to apply his emotions at the right moment and to pass the topic on to other members in a neutral way." "Individuality and a capacity for integration" allow "the various manners of expression to meld into a homogeneous whole, thereby opening up new points of view." The organizational consultant Henning Leue makes this even clearer. He distinguishes between jazz bands and traditional concert orchestras by comparing statements by Hans von Bülow, the first conductor of the Berlin Philharmonic, with those of Frederick W. Taylor. Von Bülow once said that there area no good or bad orchestras; there are only good or bad conductors. Leue claims that von Bülow's statement comes from the same line of thinking as Taylor, one of his contemporaries. Taylor demanded that "management must completely plan the activity of every worker."(Leue 1989:4). In contrast, jazz bands are showcased as exemplars of innovation-oriented cooperation: "Everyone participates, and everyone takes turns stepping into the limelight. Of course there are stars—they change the emphasis. But they are nothing without the others, and they know it. Everything is important. There is no function that can be done away with. Even small contributions are honored properly." The regulation of collective activity enjoys more freedom than it did in the Berlin orchestra at the dawn of the twentieth century, or in a Taylorist company: "There is no doubt what kind of music is being played. Even if only a few details are fixed in writing—in the selection of people, in the person doing the selecting, in the pieces and their overall stylistic arrangement, we clearly see the principles that guide the members of the band. The prescribed arrangement frees up space for individuals, who shape their own free space, improvise, refer back to familiar components, rearrange them, and invent some themselves" (Leue 1989: 3f.). What seems to make a jazz band different from a traditional orchestra is the liberty to arrange elements in such a way that they do not form a framework that cannot be upended.

The Instability of Structures: De-differentiation, De-hierarchalization, and Decentralization

Both the demand to constantly make new types of decisions and the necessity of having a free flow of information, which forms the foundation for rational and efficient decision-making, calls for "loose coupling" (Weick 1976): rationality and indeterminacy should be possible at the same time. The loose coupling concept contains an element of controllability, as well as a component that grants wide latitude. The trick is that the mechanisms of coupling and loosening do not work separately from one another: the organization no longer consists, as in Taylorism, of a firmly connected production team and a management team responsible for the requisite "loosening exercises." Instead, the principle of loose coupling should prevail at all levels. Loosely coupled organizations strive, in terms of system theory, towards high flexibility in their structures. The first use of a decision should not lead to a permanent rule for similar cases (Luhmann 2003).

The strategy of post-bureaucratic organizations aims at two things: first, the dismantling of rigid, ossified structures, and the development of a comprehensive network of loosely coupled structures. This conversion of structures is visible in three major lines in organizational strategies: the dissolution of functional differences, de-hierarchalization, and decentralization. This kind of language presumes the dismantling of bureaucratic structures. They can also assume a positive form that focuses on the integration of various areas of responsibility, democratization (or, as modern management would have it, "sociocratization"), and responsibilities situated close to the base level of the organization. Let's take a closer look at these three baselines for de-structuring (followed by restructuring).

Dissolving functional differences: All organizations are turning away from differentiation in favor of departments. These departments, as the management consultant Jürgen Fuchs says, may be competent in their field, but they are also closed off to other fields. Strict division of labor and narrow specialization led "to rigidity, to narrowing the circle of people with whom you come into contact, and to a lack of professional and personal flexibility." At the level of workers, this is said to lead to career interruptions, the development of incompetence, and midlife crises. At the overall organizational level, it leads to a style of communication similar to "lobbing things over the wall," as Fuchs puts it playfully in terms of experiences at Ford: "The design department creates a new car and then throws the design over the wall to the engineering department. They work out all the details and then throw the finished result over the wall to production. The factory changes the plans in such a way that the car can be built at a reasonable cost, and they throw the finished products over the wall to sales. So it's no surprise that the sales force also throws its cars over the wall to its customers" (Fuchs 1992: 20).

In post-bureaucratic companies, formerly divided functions are led back into production. The divisions between research, project preparation, production and marketing are eroding, as is the temporal synchronicity of work processes associated with their separation. The production area and administration are melding together. Companies hope in this way to achieve a seamless overcoming of interfaces between different areas within the work process. Work processes that were formerly divided up on a functional basis are now being located around products, or better, around processes. Employees from various company divisions that were formerly separated—such as procurement and sales, marketing, research and development, finance, and production—are now drawn together around one task, for example fulfilling a customer order or developing a new product.

De-hierarchization: The dissolution of functional differences into different departments is associated with a second fundamental development: de-hierarchization as the radical dismantling of vertical differentiation. Hierarchy is a differentiation by rank that is based on subordinated threat potential, and is typically accompanied by the differentiation of tasks and responsibilities. Hierarchies have an asymmetrical communication structure because information only flows in the form of instructions from top to bottom. Hierarchical structures imply a strict form of organization and a high degree of formal characteristics that serve as a safety mechanism against possible challenges. They form an ideology that the individual internalizes, thereby binding him to the hierarchy. Hierarchy is functional in bureaucratic, centralized organizations. It guarantees a consolidation of power, dispenses with the constant measurement of power, and liberates people from constant struggles to clarify ambiguous relationships (cf. Luhmann 1979).

The consolidation of power in hierarchies—according to the management literature—is counterproductive in turbulent, unstable environments, because this leads to decision-making programs and communication paths being fixed in place. The response to this danger is comprised, in a general way, in a drastic reduction of hierarchical levels and a rigorous increase in permeability between the remaining layers. The managers of post-bureaucratic organizations, as well as their consultants, increasingly use hierarchy in a pejorative sense.

Decentralization: The removal of vertical and horizontal differentiation leads to thorough decentralization. The processing and production of information, authority, control, and strategic planning are supposed to be situated as closely to the customer as possible. The source of value creation is relocated from own production to customers. The shift of value creation to the customer also seems to be a reaction to the displacement of demand. From the perspective of companies, customers were buying a service, not a material product. Instead of a car (which in the final analysis is nothing more than a combination of metal, plastic, glass, and electronics), an auto company sells "individual passenger transportation." Whether this service is best fulfilled by purchasing a car, or whether a combination of different services (train, bicycle, carsharing) could provision this service in a more effective and affordable way, depends not least on environmental conditions (traffic congestion, street construction, alternative offers). It is thought that the customer often doesn't want to buy a product; they want to find the solution to a problem. The fact that companies have long built their relationships with customers on the sole principle of "either buy my ready-made solution, embodied in this product, or don't buy it," reveals the limitations of this traditional thinking.

Only by proximity to the market, through technical developments, and adjustment to social change can a company meet the new maxims of speed, at least according to the ideology of corporate consultants who once championed bureaucracy and have shifted to post-bureaucracy. Companies can only gain dedication, innovation, and structural adaptability by adopting a high degree of decentralized competence (Drucker 1992: 98).

Decentralization is based in the final analysis on the assignment of autonomy and self-responsibility. Although the crème de la crème of management consultants unfortunately forget this, this autonomy can, by definition, no longer be managed centrally. Autonomous units perceive the articulations of organizational leadership as mere noise to which they are not obligated to respond. The business leadership and other autonomous units become part of the environment and, in the perception of autonomous groups, are no longer differentiated into discrete groups of customers, competitors, and state institutions. This bestows a completely new character upon communication between autonomous units within an organization, insofar as we can even speak about communication within an organization when describing cooperation between autonomous units.

More Structures and Communications

The dissolution of fixed communication paths and firmly coupled structures leads at first to an increase in new types of structural forms and communications. A trainee in a software company who is sent "on a journey" through the various areas of a firm forms a variety of different kinds of structures in the form of informal contacts; if he were integrated into the clear and transparent structures of a bureaucratic organization, this would be very different.

The fixed connections in organizational processes within bureaucratic-centralized organization "relieve" employees of the need to perform their own structuring or complex communications. Their activity could have been restricted to material projects: the composition (or disassembly) of objects, the transport of items, filling out paperwork. There are two separate fields of work: first, the work of planning, structuring, coordinating, communicating, and monitoring; and second, work that is oriented towards objects. Due to this division, organizational communication with employees was reduced on one hand to the description of the work that employees were expected to perform, and on the other hand to the distribution of wages and salaries. This is a powerfully formalized communication process. Ultimately, communication between the organization and workers consisted of payment (an invitation to continue working) or stopping payment (dismissal). Behind closed doors in the classical Taylorist organization, it was hoped that, in addition to this communication, there would be no need for further intra-organizational communication or additional organizational structuring. Under the conditions of complete stability and their acceptance by employees, the proportion of material work could theoretically be increased to one hundred percent.

The organizational scholar Henry Mintzberg describes four variables with which we can identify the character of work (1979: 222f.). The "comprehensibility of work" describes the ease with which a work process is understood. The "predictability of work" refers to the knowledge already extant within an organization that is required to execute a work process. The "diversity of work" describes the diversity of work that exists within an organization. The "speed of work" describes the speed with which the organization must react to external demands. In an organization that is oriented purely toward stability, work is completely comprehensible and predictable. Work could be planned for months, even years, in advance. The work may be complex for the organization due to the high degree of segmentation, but the assembly-line worker need only perform one or two movements. The work of the individual is therefore always the same. Because this kind of organization is based on the presumption of a stable external world, it is sufficient if reactions to possible changes are slow.

In post-bureaucratic forms of organization, the constant restructuring of organizational processes and communication about the organization of collective activity are increasingly among the main responsibilities of employees. Today, in many industrial companies, only 10 to 15 percent of employees work directly on the production of material goods. The majority of employees are occupied with research and development, management activities, maintenance and adjustment of machines, and engineering. At the same time, the number of employees in many industrial companies has risen 65 percent or more. At some high-tech companies, the 1990s saw the number of university and advanced technical college graduates exceed the number of skilled workers. A new understanding of work as communication-oriented is on the horizon.

Management literature loves the statement, "a successful organization needs three things: communication, communication, and communication," but this is as banal as it is imprecise. Communication is the foundation of all collective activity, regardless of whether we are dealing with a Taylorist or post-bureaucratic organization. The decisive point is how strongly formalized communication is. If communication in organizations is no longer formalized, then communication inevitably takes more time. This leaves less time for production-related work. If the rationalization effects that result from more communication do not compensate for the loss in time remaining for production-related work, then there is a threat that productivity will decrease.

Working from the concept of systemic rationalization, an understanding of rationalization has emerged that refers to this new significance of communication and structuring processes. Traditional corporate strategies for improvement and rationalization typically focus on the review and change of operating processes so that the given factors of operating production can be better combined for the purpose of increasing profits. In Taylorist and bureaucratic-centralized companies, rationalization strategies focus first on the technical-organizational production system (mechanization, automation, integration of information technology, increasing flexibility, logistics); second, on the organization of work (changing the horizontal and vertical division of labor, forms of cooperation, organizational control of day-to-day work); and third, on the alignment of employees to the company's requirements. Systemic rationalization, on the other hand, assigns less focus to optimizing the performance of discrete production processes and the capacity utilization of specific systems; instead, this approach places more weight on the optimal coordination of individual processes. The aim here is to combine already extensively optimized individual services into an innovative, harmonious whole.

3.3 The Structure of Post-bureaucratic Organizations

Decentralization, de-hierarchalization, and the deformalization of communication: this is the direction in which post-bureaucratic organizations are heading. The new principles are clear: no internal or external boundaries, structures that are readily open to change, loose couplings, and combined systems of independent performance centers. But what exactly do coordination mechanisms look like in post-bureaucratic organizations? Which internal form of organization corresponds most closely to the demands of constant change? New concepts sprinkled with great-sounding buzz words such as "Lean Management," "fractal factory," "circular company," "agile organization," and "post-modern factory" all have one thing in common: at their core is the organization of project groups and semi-autonomous work groups.

Quality Circles, Semi-autonomous Work Teams, and Project Groups

The names used for teams have a superlative, exaggerating quality. They are described as quality circles, innovation discussion groups, workshop control groups, action groups, problem-solving groups, participation initiatives, proposal groups, production teams, modules, tribes, and cells, and every year we see several new and fashionable descriptions for teams. In this jungle of nomenclature, there are roughly three types of teams; we will call them the quality circle, semi-autonomous work groups, and project groups.

Quality circles are a management system for improving the productivity and quality of products and services. This is supposed to be done by means of developing and motivating workers and improving their working life (Vaziri 1987: 17). These are typically groups of six to ten employees who meet regularly and voluntarily. The participants mostly come from the same division and meet under the leadership of a moderator. They identify shared work-related problems, look for solutions, and introduce them into the work process. The idea behind the quality circle is the principle that it is better to "produce" quality than to "monitor" it. This means that quality should be shifted into the responsibilities of employees in production.

Quality circles are an instrument for optimizing centralized-bureaucratic organizations along the lines of "participative Taylorism" (cf. Linhart 1991: 81). These circles are not a method for structuring work; instead, they are a parallel organization that can be easily integrated, for instance in assembly-line work. Circles have the right to make proposals, but they do not have any decision-making authority. Decision-makers who held this responsibility previously therefore retain their authority. Circles are not tasked with developing concepts; they only address the details of retrospective improvements. In this way, they do not pose a competitive threat to technical planning departments or project preparation groups; they merely assume a complementary function for dealing with problems that would be too difficult to solve at different levels.

In contrast, semi-autonomous work groups—including semi-autonomous production groups in industry—grant workers a high degree of autonomy and control over their immediate work behaviors. The workers in these groups have a broad spectrum of tasks, including activities that traditionally fall within management's remit. They order materials, determine overtime hours, decide who takes what work position, define job rotations, calculate productivity, monitor a budget, and both hire and fire employees.

Teamwork played a central role in Lean Management, which was the darling of corporate managers for a long time.[13] Only the rigorous application of group work was said to enable the attainment of an ambitious goal: high flexibility in fabrication and maximization of quality. Increased flexibility was supposed to make production efficient, even for smaller production batches. Assembly workers were supposed to take on the adjustment, conversion, maintenance, and repair of machines themselves. In the context of Total Quality Management, they strive to attain the highest degree of quality by means of a constant process of problem-solving and fault correction (Kaizen). A proactive, constant quality assurance process in terms of products and production is meant to render all rework superfluous, as well as enable a product that corresponds largely to the zero-error standard. The potential for flexibility and quality that inheres to Lean Management could, according to the rhetoric of the time, only be tapped by means of a comprehensive rationalization of the organization of work. Formerly outsourced divisions, such as quality assurance, rework, machine repair and maintenance, were supposed to return to the fold of a company's own production process. At the center of Lean Production stood work teams that were led by strong leadership personalities.

A third type, the *project group*, can also be distinguished in addition to quality circles and semi-autonomous work groups. Project groups are bound to a special event or temporary objective. The tasks of a project group are often not clearly fixed; instead, they are defined in detail independently by the project group. The project groups then disband after attaining a specific goal (or upon realizing that the goal is not attainable). They are distinguished from semi-autonomous production groups by the fact that they are generally exposed to a "rationality dilemma." The actors in a project group find themselves in a situation with double responsibilities. They are responsible for the success of the project group, but also have to attend to the duties of the unit that assigned them to the group.

Project groups, semi-autonomous work groups, and with some limitations quality circles as well, show that the application of new kinds of organizational forms can put us in a position to react to external uncertainty; however, this also leads to an increase in internal uncertainty. Teams can react better to a turbulent environment thanks to their increased flexibility, but to do so they give up their structure of fixed connections. New structures emerge in everyday work, but they have less consistency. The entire organization profits from this constant restructuring, because it leads—at least in theory—to the unleashing of all of the potential that exists within a group. The organization can tap into otherwise idle knowledge held by workers and employees and make it useful. On the other hand, however, the workers also stand to gain from restructuring because it means constant re-training. Work processes are modified again and again, which entails learning. Work that was previously exposed to a steady process of de-skilling, especially in assembly-line work, becomes valuable again.

The formation of groups has existed for quite some time in organizations. German and American industry were already experimenting in the early twentieth century with work groups integrated into the formal structure of companies. And even in the most Taylorized companies—as the human relations approach in organizational science has shown—work groups had formed at the informal level as cliques with their own customs, obligations, routines and rituals (cf. Mayo 1948: 128). The roles and responsibilities in these informal cliques are limited however to the simplification and redefinition of the movements prescribed by production planning, and to the formation of collective resistance again management measures that are deemed unjustified (cf. Luhmann 1964: 324ff.).

In contrast to these disparate islands of formal groups existing within the organization, and the informal cliques arising in the shadow of formal structures, groups in post-bureaucratic organizations are no longer a byproduct, disdained by management, of an organization structured from the top down. They have become instead the basic unit of collective activity. This is why the "functioning" of semi-autonomous work groups and project groups is seen as essential for, perhaps even as an existential condition of, an organization's success.

Connecting Autonomous Units

When establishing teams as the central form of internal (and increasingly external as well) coordination, the organization stands before the dilemma of having to interlace individual, relative autonomous group units horizontally and—if hierarchies were to be upheld—vertically. If, as the wise old man among US-American management consultants, Peter F. Drucker, claims, the ponderous battleship "company" should be replaced by an agile organization of smaller, more maneuverable craft, this raises the question of how the individual ships in the "Action Company 1999" fleet are supposed to communicate and cooperate (cf. Drucker 1990). The problem for organizations lies in how cooperation between the groups can function without impairing the free flow of information between the units and the teams' extensive autonomy.

It sounds nice and post-bureaucratic whenever managers are supposed to uphold the dynamism of the organization and its employees by means of "an open climate of communication with feedback mechanisms, flexible project organization, and network structures." And everyone agrees that "organizational assets," the "expertise of employees," cannot come into its own in a framework of "rigid hierarchies and narrow rules." Successful strategies, however, have to go beyond these narratives of social humanity, no matter how beloved they are in organizations.

The American futurologist Alvin Toffler pointed out a possible instrument of regulation as early as the 1970s. In the adhocracies that he observed, the contact between autonomous units was upheld through informal relationships. Informal relationships guarantee a critically important communication network in view of the churning within adhocracies, with titles, jobs and responsibilities changing, structures collapsing and rising, departments and project groups being born and buried, all at breakneck speed (Toffler 1971). These relationships are said to be the lifeline of adhocracies. This is revealed by the fact that most organizations would fall to pieces if everyone worked exclusively according to plan. If air traffic controllers, policemen, or physicians went on a slow-down strike and only did their jobs according to the bare minimum for a few months, then the organization would quickly come to a standstill.

Post-bureaucratic organizations attempt to promote the formation of informal systems in a targeted way. By changing teams, groups can be loosely connected and form a network of flexible structures. Constantly changing the members of work groups and project groups is meant to create a complex web of communication and cooperation. Coordination problems then do not exist between the individual groups, but the topics of conflict become who works when and for how long in which projects. Throughout the life of the projects, then, fixed structures are not created, but personal relationships emerge that people can refer back to for general organizational coordination. People profit from the fact that purely personal relationships become loose mechanisms of coordination and communication.

If we think it through to its logical conclusion, the relatively promising connection of autonomous subunits could be attained by developing relationships of love and friendship beyond the confines of groups. In this sense, a post-bureaucratic organization would also always have to be a dating agency. Organizations would probably refuse to identify matchmaking as a goal alongside the maximization of profit, the winning of votes, or the waging of war. However, this refusal cannot be fully persuasive, which is why the (mostly!) successful principle of coordination by familial clans—"management by love"—should also not be deployed in the somewhat looser form of friendships and relationships in post-bureaucratic organizations.

Dense network structures are supposed to emerge in organizations from informal communication. The various work units that form a network should take up contact with all groups and individuals with whom they have to communicate, thereby producing a dense and transparent network of information, understandings, and agreements. In Peter F. Drucker's "factory of 1999," all of the groups, project teams, and departments were supposed to reflect on what information they owed to whom and what information people needed from others. A significant portion of information would flow horizontally, beyond the boundaries of departments and groups. The factory of 1999 was supposed to be an information network in which all of the managers have to understand and be familiar with the entire process. Like the members of individual teams, they had to be in the know and act and remain oriented to business performance. Above all, they had to ask themselves: what do the leaders of other modules need to know about the characteristics, capacities, plans, and work methods of my unit? And, vice versa, what information do we actually need from others? (Warnecke 1993).

It is considered important in this constellation that the relationships between different groups of a network are always subjected to critical scrutiny. As soon as there is coercion towards cooperation, a network would degenerate into a bureaucratic organization. This is why increasing numbers of organizations are moving towards allowing certain internal groups (for example, training, consulting) to compete against external providers in a market within the organization. A semi-autonomous work group's option to procure consulting from outside the organization is supposed to dispel the otherwise extant fixed connection between the value creation group and the internal team for training and consulting. This mechanism is supposed to work even in vertical coordination relationships. A work group that is highly autonomous can at least theoretically issue a threat to management that it will become independent or seek other, more suitable, management. This threat potential puts the relationship between semi-autonomous work groups and central management on shaky ground, thereby contributing to the dissolution of an otherwise extremely strong fixed structure. Even if connections to businesses and places, organization-specific qualifications, lack of capital, or insufficient willingness to take on risks may render this option a purely theoretical one in many cases, it still has effects on relations between management and relatively autonomous organization centers.

Network structures based on informal relationships are important instruments for connecting autonomous units with one another. Even if networks are praised to the heavens in management rhetoric, the actual trust placed in informal networks within organizations is in many cases not especially great. This is why most decentralized pioneer organizations frequently develop variations on the classical hierarchical model of organization. "Participative management," "service pyramids," and "sociocracy" are methods that in the final analysis do not rely completely on the ability of informal systems and networks to organize themselves. Instead, these approaches include moderated hierarchical structures in organizational networks.

Participative management should, according to the ideas of more or less post-bureaucratic organization consultants, guarantee the inclusion of as many employees as possible in vertical hierarchical coordination. The supervisor, if this term even continues to exist, is transformed from a commanding person of authority to a host and moderator. This person has to create a trusting relationship between herself and her employees and facilitate their inclusion in decision-making processes (cf. Crozier 1989: 64). The striking thing about participative management is that it does not do away with hierarchy as a means of vertical coordination. It involves but does not empower. Charles Perrow, one of the leading American organizational theorists, criticized participative management decades ago as a "hygienic spray": people may strive to reduce the feeling of alienation among employees, yet the power that is granted to them is extremely limited. They would be included in an advisory capacity for decision-making, and also encouraged to make certain decisions themselves. These decisions could however always be subject to veto. This would be comparable with a democratic system in which people would elect their own leaders, although the leaders could declare the election invalid. Perrow assumes that participative management would give employees and workers a voice, and would improve the quality of decisions. The decisions, however, would remain—whatever the level of participation—decisions made by management (Perrow 1974: 35).

The idea of the *service pyramid* promoted the inversion of the hierarchic principle from above and below, at least on the display side of an organization. Hierarchical leadership, according to Jan Carlzon (1987), former head of the Scandinavian airline SAS, should become a service to which the employees have a right and a claim. In the inverted pyramid model, the customers are at the very top, followed by the employees who have direct contact with customers, followed by management and the board of directors. The service pyramid may be impressive in its visual clarity and its contrast to conventional hierarchical pyramids, but it does not solve the problem of coordination. This approach remains vague about what interest the uppermost teams and employees would have in maintaining this pyramid, as well as why they should pay for this service. And lastly, it conceals the fact that the "hierarchical service provider" can always intervene in the form of a decree to access "their customers."

This accounts for the popularity of models that claim to resolve the dilemma that arises between the necessity of vertical coordination between teams and the concession of higher autonomy. In a *sociocracy* or holacracy, "the typical command-obey mechanism" is supposed to be broken, with the need for coordination and monitoring covered by just a few fundamental rules. Every one and every position is determined by a vote. Duplicated connections are vertically lined up with one another. In this process, every team is represented doubly in the next higher team by a functional leader (manager) and an elected representative (Buck/Endenburg 1984: 5). All decisions are made on the basis of consensus, whereby consensus doesn't always mean approval by all; consensus can also be taken as the non-existence of opposition. Ultimately, the consensus principle gives employees the security that nothing can be decided against their will.

Despite the Enthusiasm: Initial Doubts and Questions

The more certain the end of the classical bureaucratic, hierarchical organization, the more daring the proposals presented to the public by organizational consultants. Whoever follows the crème de la crème of German, French, American, Japanese, and Chinese organizational consultants to promote "integrative-innovative companies," "System 5," "Theory Z," "multicellular organizations," Flex Firms," "Lean Companies," "fractal factories," "cellular systems," "ambidextrous companies," or "agile organizations," will not be content with a just a bit of participative management, team work, and project organization. While people used to be satisfied with a bit more motivation and customer service orientation here, and slightly more efficient communication channels there, today people are daring to try out ambitious, comprehensive management approaches. This leads to announcements of big successes, both in the past and today.

As the Reengineering gurus Michael Hammer and James Champy (1993) showed in the 1990s, you had to promise a "business revolution" that left no stone unturned to even get managers interested. In comparison to Hammer and Champy, who promised improvements on the order of ten times previous performance, the godfathers of Lean Management—James P. Womack, Daniel T. Jones und Daniel Roos (1991)—seem altogether modest; they only promised to double productivity while simultaneously reducing costs and headcount by half. Lean Management and Reengineering owed their triumph among the upper echelons of managers, as did those of similarly peppy-sounding management concepts, to the fact that they offered an integrative approach that was supposed to remedy all of the worries, large and small, of an organization's leadership. The panacea of Lean Management or Reengineering promised to replace the patchwork fixes for specific symptoms. Instead of having to confront the individual fields of simultaneous product development, just-in-time logistics, technology planning, personnel development, teamwork, Total Quality Management, and decentralized production structures, everything was now subsumed under a catchy motto.[14]

Whether Lean Management, Flex Firm, multicellular companies, fractal factories, or agile organizations—all of these models present themselves as conclusive and tout all-encompassing solutions that leave outsiders breathless. A solution of striking simplicity seems to be found or invented by management consultants each and every week. If everything that lean, reengineered, or post-bureaucratic organizations bought as their new organizational structure actually existed, then we could justifiably—indeed, we would be compelled to—talk about a veritable revolution. Under the guiding maxim of innovation ability, project organizations connected like networks would react flexibly and quickly to rapidly changing environmental conditions. New kinds of networks, intermediary forms of markets and organization, would break up the rigidity of hierarchical organization and help to structure a turbulent external world. Employees would be the winners of the revolution and become the new rulers in know-how organizations in which material work would be largely replaced by communications, planning and structuring activities.

But questions began cropping up for me in the description of the discourse among new management gurus and a few employees of post-bureaucratic organizations: How can autonomous units be combined into a harmonious whole? Can management and self-organization be brought into accord? Is participative management compatible with de-hierarchalization? Can the inverted service pyramid be more than just a pretty picture?

Post-bureaucratic management consultants and organizational leaders typically hail from the bureaucratic, Taylorist tradition and therefore seem, casually speaking, bowled over by the new freedoms presented on the display side of post-bureaucratic organizations. What is sold today under a broad array of names as new forms of organization is, however, not too far distant from what has been tried out in democratic or autonomous groups for several years already, and with significant problems. Organizations that preach the slogan, "change is the only true constant," have to answer the same questions and doubts as anarchistic groups that have subscribed to absolute freedom under the motto, "no power for anyone."

4.
The Dilemmas of
Post-bureaucratic Organizations

Freedom is not possible without order
And order without freedom has no value.
Mahatma Gandhi

Assessments of post-bureaucratic organizations in the financial press, the management literature, and often in organizational science as well, are frequently distinguished by a surprising lack of critique. The fact that organizations present themselves as something special in their self-descriptions is understandable, perhaps even necessary; an attractive display side serves to stabilize internal organizational cohesion and the boundaries with the outside world. But management consultants who are paid for the critical review of organizations—at least according to theory and their consulting contracts—seem almost to have found a new doctrine of salvation in the concept of the post-bureaucratic organization. Management magazines, which with their tendency to dramatize new developments are always hunting for new management methods, contribute significantly to the glorification of new organizational concepts (see Jung/Kieser 2012). And even respected social scientists such as Michel Crozier (1989), the doyen of French organizational sociology, do not hesitate to join in the chorus of hallelujahs for new forms of organization.

However, even if we do not trust the proscenium—the display side—of post-bureaucratic organizations, choosing instead to construct the backstage with more precision with the aid of central insights from organizational science, then we stumble upon fundamental problems that have not yet been resolved. The problem of post-bureaucratic organizations is located less in resistance from middle management to the loss of positions or the inability of workers to adjust to new demands.[15] Instead, the orientation towards change, flexibility, and innovation drives post-bureaucratic organizations literally to the edge of their existential possibilities. Post-bureaucratic organizations therefore stand before the fundamental problem of holding together an organization oriented towards innovation and the ability to change (Section 4.1). De-hierarchalization does not lead to a "workers' revolution"—in which workers assume central functions of power and decision-making—but rather to intensifying power struggles in organizations (Section 4.2). The streamlining of organizational processes, which are supposed to lead to a reduction of increasing complexity, actually have the opposite effect, leading to more complex and less transparent processes (Section 4.3). Organizations that change themselves confront the following dilemma: in the face of growing demands for flexibility, there is no going back to Taylorist, bureaucratic forms of organization; however, loose connections expose post-bureaucratic organizations to a fundamental danger of "dissolution" and "politicization."

4.1 The Identity Dilemma: The (Necessary) Limits of Organizations

Even in the most post-bureaucratic of the post-bureaucratic organizations, there is a tendency towards rules, routines, stability, and redundancy. Burns and Stalker (1966) as well as Mintzberg (1988) have observed that even the most committed members of adhocracies sometimes displayed a truly low tolerance for insecurity, uncertainty, and disorder. In certain situations, according to the organizational theorists Burns and Stalker, some managers in adhocracies cry out in desperation for more order and structure. As the following will show, this is caused by an inherent tendency within post-bureaucratic organizations for self-dissolution.

Organizations, whether they are pre-bureaucratic, bureaucratic, or post-bureaucratic, are not natural phenomena; they are artificial constructs. Their existence and their continued existence is always under threat, a point on which action theory (Crozier/Friedberg 1977) and systems theory (Luhmann 2000) are in agreement. In post-bureaucratic organizations, the general endangerment of existence and continued existence is a ubiquitous problem. The more loosely connected organizations are, the less protective mechanisms they have against the individual, limited rationalities of their members. The larger the palette of possibilities in an organization, the more likely it is that the local rationalities of organization members can assert themselves against the organization's logic. The continuous increase in the ability to change can lead ultimately to the dissolution of the organization. There is a danger that the organization can lose its inner cohesion in the face of so many possibilities (contingency). What is lost is the defining feature of organizations: their delimitation from the outside world. Organizations are exposed to the danger of "coming apart" when they are integrated with an uncertain environment and when they grant autonomy to their employees.

Organizations on their Way to the Land of Unlimited Opportunities

The fundamental problem of post-bureaucratic organizations—the drawing of boundaries with the external world—can be understood in terms of organizational sociology with the aid of systems theory. Organizations distinguish themselves from their environment by limiting the range of possibilities. Organizations—or, more generally speaking, systems—are structured relational constructs that establish certain possibilities and exclude others. In turbulent environments, there is always a surfeit of possibilities. This means that organizations are forced to sort things out by means of decisions. They are required to defend for their own sake their section of the world—meaning their own finiteness—against the "constant threat of other possibilities" (Luhmann 1969: 395). To put it differently, systems only exist by virtue of the fact that they have a lower contingency than their environment. They can only obtain their identity through this difference between their own finiteness and their omnipotent environment (cf. Luhmann 1984: 242f.).

Finiteness is created by drawing a boundary: "something is what it is only in its limit and by virtue of its own limit" (Hegel). The limit grants the "something" its existence. Drawing a limit to the external world is done by meaningfully ordering internal structures and processes. An organization can decide, by means of drawing limits, which actions are "in their meaning" and which are not.[16] Meaning is a necessary selection criterion for reducing environmental complexity and deciding which elements should be connected to one another.[17] An organization's meaning has a controlling effect as a network of selection rules: environmental conditions are typified, the current status is distinguished from what is possible, and the world is seen in a specific way. This meaning-related selection is established by traditions, forms in the processing with expectations from the environment, and determines the internal differentiation of organizations.

This internal differentiation is nothing other than the structure of an organization. Meaningful selection and interior structuring depends on how the organization understands its differentiation with the exterior world. If an economic organization, for example, suddenly stops striving for more profitability (or preservation of solvency) and begins pursuing religious fulfillment, ideological propriety, moral uprightness, or the realization of eternal truths, then we can assume with considerable certainty that we will have to deal with confusion in meaningful selection mechanisms.[18] In this respect, business organizations must strive for two things. First, they must retain the criterion of economic efficiency as a centrally meaningful mechanism of selection, because otherwise they would cease to be an "economic" organization. Second, they must apply this selection mechanism to differentiate from the environment, because otherwise they would cease to be an economic "organization."

This connection of elements, processes, and structures into one system is generally variable. To put it differently, meaning as a point of control for these system formations is unstable. For example, meaning can be altered due to changing environmental conditions. Systems—and in special cases organizations—are therefore constructs that are both identified in terms of meaning and that generate meaning. On one hand, social systems arise on the foundation of meaning as a guiding criterion in the selective association of elements, and they are in this regard constituted by meaning. On the other hand, it is possible for social systems, on the basis of their contingency, to forge new relational links, to create new meaning from them, and therefore have a meaning-constituting effect. Because meaning, as a means of delimiting systems from their environment, is protean, the limits between the system and environment are also variable: A system is its differentiation to the environment; it is a limit-defining, limit-upholding order (Luhmann 1975b: 221).

These limits have the "double function of separating and connecting system and environment" (Luhmann 1984: 52; English translation Luhmann 1995, p. 46). They stabilize the system by delimiting a system's elements from the environment. At the same time, these limits also permit the relations between the system and its environment, enabling the exchange of information and material and thereby serving the system's transformability. The formation of limits is conducive both to preserving the system as well as exchanging with other systems. These limits resemble cell membranes that close the cell off and can also open at the same time for exchange relationships with other cells.

What happens now, if we find an ideally conceived organization that has managed, with the aid of the best organizational consultations, to produce an infinitude of variance, in order to meet the demand from some quarters to become a limitless organization? The limits between system and environment would disappear, in the truest sense of the word. The process of meaning selection of decisions would be terminated. The organization would degenerate into a mere mass of scarcely cohesive decisions. It would no longer be possible to reduce the complexity of the world to a dimension that can be handled internally; the orientation and processing performance of the system would drop to zero immediately. The complete abolition of redundancy would disable the mechanism for producing decisions. Total flexibility would lead the organization to lose its feeling for unity and continuity. "Chronic flexibility" would destroy identity (Weick 1979). The organization would thereby lose its mechanism for delimiting itself from the environment. Then it would flow into the environment, so to speak, and would disintegrate in the realm of unlimited possibilities. The transposition of external uncertainty into internal uncertainty therefore brings along the danger of destroying the essence of an organization.

The Problem of Delimitation: Blurry Boundaries Between the Organization and its Environment

Yet those organizations that have not committed to complete change are still subjected to the same misery, even if at a less fundamental level. To put it simply, this is the "problem" of blurring the boundaries between the environment and organizations, or the fact that post-bureaucratic organizations only have a thin, permeable, porous limits to the exterior world (Peters 1988b: 661).

The use of market mechanisms in internal organization processes and the organization of market processes makes it more difficult to set limits between organizations and the environment. In Taylorist bureaucratic organizations, hierarchical regulation was the means of organizing internal processes. Environmental relations took place through market mechanisms. As we saw in the previous chapters, the mechanisms of intra- and inter-organizational communication and coordination begin to interweave in post-bureaucratic organizations. The constantly threatening self-dissolution of post-bureaucratic organizations, and the blurring of boundaries between the environment and the organization, becomes concrete in all areas of organizations in which mechanisms are set for innovation and flexibility. This becomes clear in central areas such as relationships to other organizations, the territorial definition of the organization, and the definition of organization membership.

Relationships to suppliers, customers, agencies, and the public are no longer monopolized in one organizational area in post-bureaucratic organizations. This potentially allows every employee to make use of these openly designed environmental relationships. The beloved maxims of post-bureaucratic organizations, such as "our goal is to give the customer what he wants, when he wants it," or "if you want things to be done, just do it," legitimate, even demand, that individual employees take up contacts with other organizations. This clearly makes it more difficult to draw limits between the organization and the environment, became environmental contacts are no longer channeled through clearly defined "border stations."

The more the inner structures assume a fluid state—parallel to the dissolution of clear limits—and the more labile the organizational scaffolding becomes, the greater the threat of dissolution looms before an organization (cf. Powell 2007: 507). The reaction to such symptoms of diffusion—and here organizations do not differ much from states—is typically a hardening of internal structures: authoritarian rules, clear lines of responsibility, and more pronounced internal structuring. The dilemma of post-bureaucratic organizations lies in the fact that these reactions may stabilize the organization internally, but they reduce the flexibility of contact to the environment.

One expression of the danger of diffusion for post-bureaucratic organizations is the increasing difficulty of determining territoriality. The post-bureaucratic organization becomes an "organization without a country." Activities in post-bureaucratic companies take place with increasing frequency outside of the head office. Value creation occurs more "directly at the customer"—outside of the company. "Outside of the company": this observation alone makes it clear how much an organization is usually defined in terms of a place or territory. It was easy to "locate" an organization and its membership in the age of Taylorist bureaucracy. A "workplace" guaranteed that employees would always be found at the same place. The "positions" revealed the location of functions in the organization; the names of companies or of administrative centers also denoted the building in which production or administration was performed. In post-bureaucratic organizations, these means of characterization are annulled as it becomes increasingly difficult to identify the geographical boundaries of an organization.

We also find an increasing ambiguity about who can and cannot belong to an organization, paralleled by a growing difficulty of ascertaining an organization's location. The definition of membership and non-membership in an organization is central for the definition of formal systems of organization, as Luhmann pointed out decades ago (cf. Luhmann 1964: 39ff.; Luhmann 1969: 395). The clear determination of membership ensures predictability for the members, the organization, and the environment. People can demand that members behave in accordance with certain expectations for their roles, and members can rely on the fact that more will not be expected of them than was set out in a catalogue of expectations (for example, in a job description). This general predictability disappears in post-bureaucratic organizations; an employee in an autonomous production group cannot be included in the overall organization without further ado. The manager in a profit center does not have to have much to do with employees in other profit centers than with the employees in completely different companies. A consultant working on a fee basis for corporate consulting cannot be counted clearly to an organization's interior or exterior environment. The clear "member or non-member" scheme in Taylorist-bureaucratic companies—which is central to determining the limits of an organization—is replaced by increasingly complex relationships between people and organizations.

This ever more complex relationships are expressed in growing problems with loyalty. In the moment at which we ask employees to identify more strongly with their professional responsibilities, their work team, or with the tasks entrusted to them by customers, these employees' loyalty to the entire organization tends to decrease (Knoke 2001: 170ff.). If workers are fully responsible for a business unit, then the well-being of their unit will at some point become more important than the well-being of the entire organization. If the employees work in an independent team, it is not clear to them why they should pitch in when there are capacity bottlenecks in other organization areas.

Intensification of Departmental Self-interest

We can understand why there are constant complaints about "departmental self-interest" in post-bureaucratic organizations. It is certainly regrettable that a trend towards "narrow-minded sectionalism" arises from the division into largely autonomous units, which prevents the necessary exchange of knowledge, experience, and information. Yet when creating largely independent, autonomous organizational units, we also run the risk that they will take advantage of these opportunities. The problem—namely that autonomous units only identify themselves to a limited degree with the entire organization—is the not a byproduct of poor decentralization, but rather the result of the resolute development of independent units.

Post-bureaucratic organizations are constantly struggling with the trend towards independence evident in these groups, with intensifying rivalries between units over ever-scarcer central resources and with constant disputes over authority between central managers and managers of autonomous units. Admittedly, these identity problems are not completely new. Even in classical, hierarchical, bureaucratic organizations, departments had their own identities, and there were disputes over authority and jurisdiction, as well as the problem of integrating all of this in an organization for the purpose of pursuing a goal. The powerful position of the upper organization, however, constituted an entity that had relatively expansive competences for solving these problems. In post-bureaucratic organizations, the head office only has very limited access to these competences. When we look at some particularly advanced post-bureaucratic organizations, we can see these problems as if we were looking through a magnifying glass. To name just five examples:

Product offering: If we are to believe claims by companies, as well as administrations, then increasing numbers of customers expect complete solutions for comprehensive problems, not just the satisfaction of a specific, selective need. But it is precisely this profit center structure of many decentralized organizations that runs counter to this demand for system solutions and complete solutions. The unbundling of a company or an administration into several autonomous units, each directed at a single effort, requires complex re-coordination between the individual units to be able to generate complete offers. Where clear instructions from the organization's leaders once sufficed, now complicated bilateral or multilateral negotiations have to take place.

Synergy effects: The integration of tasks and functions in decentralized organizations involves the fact that competences are no longer concentrated at one place in the organization; instead, they are situated in various organizational units. Instead of being located in central departments such as research, development, human resources, or sales, these functions are moved to individual profit centers. Instead of having central departments for project planning, production planning, and quality assurance, these functions are given to semi-autonomous groups. This leads to the danger that the same competences will be built up at different points inside an organization. Achieving synergy effects, such as the shared use of organizational resources, becomes more improbable and has to be ensured by means of intensive coordination processes.

Innovation: In management, there is often a tendency to favor product innovations that are easy to accept, do not pose any major risks, and do not require major adjustments in the organization. This tendency towards a modest innovation policy is further intensified through a division into autonomous units. Basic innovations incur such high costs for development and launch, and require such long initial phases, that many autonomous units do not take this risk on. This means that increasing decentralization may lead to stronger product innovation policy at the small level, but it also means that comprehensive, cost-intensive innovations become all the more unlikely. If the organization wants to facilitate such extensive innovations, then coordination processes will be necessary between the units.

Reorganizations: Comprehensive reorganizations become increasingly difficult to implement in decentralized organizations. The head of the organization can only hold independent units fully responsible for their business results if these units have broad autonomy in designing the organization of their work. This impedes extensive restructuring efforts because they would call the independence of units into question. Organizational governance that sets down the organizational changes that the leaders of the individual units have to implement cannot make these leaders fully responsible for organizational results. On the other hand, the departments that were responsible for organization and reorganization in the former, functionally organized structure, are increasingly integrated into the individual product-oriented units. This means that organizational heads scarcely have any units at their disposal through which a major reorganization could be carried out. For example, there are indicators that shifting project planning functions into semi-autonomous groups leads to a situation in which these groups can scarcely take on changes of a fundamental nature. And third, organizational changes cause fewer domino effects in decentralized forms of organizations. If organizational units are closely connected to each other, then a major change in one unit typically leads to changes in the other units. In an organizational that is clearly structured along functional lines, this makes it easier for the management to implement fundamental changes that affect the entire organization. In a decentralized organization, the units are only loosely connected with one another. This results in the fact that fundamental changes in one organizational unit no longer leads necessarily to immediate changes in another unit.

Procurement: The comprehensive, organization-wide use of resources and a strong presence on the procurement market were an important argument for a functional organization. Splitting an organization up into autonomous segments threatens to abolish this synergy effect. There is a danger that every unit would purchase products from suppliers at excessive prices. While a larger organization's uniform presence on the procurement market places significant power potential on the side of the organization, non-coordinated procurement can enable suppliers to play organizational units off against one another, thereby significantly increasing their power.

In view of the new challenges for coordination sketched out here, it becomes clear that the management of post-bureaucratic organizations confront a dilemma: the head office has the paradoxical task of granting autonomy to organizational units, yet at the same it must ensure that the individual units identify with the organization's overall aims. Managers have to facilitate disintegration into autonomous units, while simultaneously finding means for integrating autonomous units into the overall organization. The contrast between autonomy and independence in business units on one hand, and the integration and self-incorporation of the entire organization on the other, becomes a dilemma in post-bureaucratic organizations.

The constant danger that organizational forms oriented towards flexibility and change will come undone in the realm of unlimited possibilities places post-bureaucratic organizations before a central task: how can we take account of the demand for change without dissolving outwards or inwards? How can we prevent divergence in a post-bureaucratic organization that has been adapted to a turbulent environment? How can internal organizational uncertainty be reduced in such a way that it does not impact the capacity for change? What possibilities are there for fixed structures that do not have an innovation-inhibiting effect? How can flexibility and the standardization required for managing a system be brought together?

The identity dilemma of post-bureaucratic organizations consists of the granting of maximum autonomy to independent organizational units while at the same time integrating these autonomous units in such a way that the entire organization retains a full-fledged identity. This dilemma develops substantial explosiveness because the increasing orientation towards flexibility literally pushes the organization to the edge of its viability, yet, due to technical revolutions, there is no going back to a purely stability-oriented organization that is equipped with a clear identity. Instead of the following the maxim, "change is the only constant," new kinds of organizations must find ways to cut through this almost Gordian knot.

4.2 The Politicization Dilemma: Power Struggles in Post-bureaucratic Organizations

If we were to invest our trust in the display side of post-bureaucratic organizations, then their employees are "the new rulers": the "well-being and needs" of the organization depends on them. The employees are said to "no longer be an employee in the traditional sense"; they are "actually employers." They are said to give "their work, their performance, their service to the customer" (Fuchs 1992: 59ff.). The rise of employees from "wage-earners to productive service partners" would lead, according to the claims of many post-bureaucratic organizations, to egalitarian power relations.

If, as we discussed in the previous chapter, we cannot be dealing with a revolutionary transformation from the principle of stability to one of flexibility and change, then attentive readers of the current management literature may harbor the hope—inspired by the almost religious fervor with which these claims are frequently made—that at least the power relations within post-bureaucratic organizations could have undergone revolutionary change. This raises the question of whether, after the the "manager revolution" of the 1940s, in which internal company power shifted from equity owners to managers who did not hold equity (cf. Burnham 1941), we are now seeing an "employee revolution." What is there to the thesis of workers as the "new powers" in organizations?

If the employees of post-bureaucratic organizations are truly the "new rulers," then this raises questions of a fundamental nature. This is why management, the "old rulers," does not suddenly give up its central position, relinquish control over work processes, and thereby consciously surrender to the dependency of employees and workers. Why would the decades-long struggle between management and employees over control of the company suddenly be decided in favor of the employees? Why is management of all things the driving motor for this development? Why are the efforts at humanization and democratization, against which organizational leadership has struggled and sought to prevent for so long, suddenly being promoted as part of an organizational rationalization strategy?

These questions raise doubts the moment they are voiced. If we think through the rhetoric of post-bureaucratic managers and organizational consultants just a bit further, then skepticism is warranted as to whether we are really dealing with a fundamental change in power relationships. As we will see, the solution of the problems of power does not lead to general contentment, but rather to an increase in power struggles in post-bureaucratic organizations. At the same time as the identity dilemma at the organizational level, there is the dilemma of politicization at the level of mutual relationships between stakeholders.

The Benefits of Hierarchy

According to the French-Austrian sociology team of Michel Crozier and Erhard Friedberg (1977: 72), power is based on zones of uncertainty that are relevant to control. This means that power, in its internal logic, works with potential threats; the threat of sanctions lurks in the background. In this model, even the ostensibly "least-powerful" member of an organization wields control over zones of uncertainty, meaning that they are in a position to "make a difference" for the partners with whom they interact (Giddens 1982: 197). Power relationships in organizations are asymmetrical. Power is a correlation of forces, out of which one can always pull more than the others, yet in which no one is fully at anyone else's mercy. Power represents a relationship of exchange in which one of the systems involved (mental or organizational) is in a position to impose upon others conditions of exchange that are favorable to the more powerful system. This "relational theory of power" (Crozier/Friedberg 1977: 65f.) assumes that power is a basic dimension of social action. Power relationships are formed precisely because human beings are free and relatively autonomous.

Hierarchies therefore arise whenever power relationships are consolidated and stabilized, and all of the members have to demonstrate their attachments to hierarchies, at least in their official self-representation. The consolidation of power relationships in organizations therefore takes place at a very central level through the formalization of structures, especially of communication paths. The formalization of hierarchical communication paths enables managers to wield control over central zones of uncertainty—decisions about whether a member remains in the organization (exit power) and often over their advancement (career power) (cf. Kühl 2013: 65ff. with reference to Luhmann 1979).

Hierarchies were accepted for a long time and without critique as the central mechanism of control and coordination for organizations, both in capitalist and socialist societies. Aside from isolated attempts at democratization in the second half of the twentieth century, hierarchy was *the* management instrument for connecting complex work processes and decision-making with one another. Acceptance was not limited just to the upper managers and the actual hierarchies themselves. The majority of employees, whose operational role was restricted to the receipt of instructions and their execution, also accepted the central importance of hierarchical command structures. Hierarchy, which literally means "sacred order," lived up to its name in operational practice.

Even if hierarchy had a negative aftertaste, there is a good reason for its attractiveness as a mechanism of management and coordination. Authority as hierarchy secures, in a relatively convincing way, the decidability of problems, which is a central task in organizations. This is associated with their central characteristic: hierarchy generates the decidability of problems in that it develops a generally accepted system of people who issue instructions and people who follow them, and this enables the development of value-creation processes that are structured in a powerfully collaborative way. The hierarch can resolve open decisions by referring to his role as the boss. As a superior in the hierarchy, it is possible for him to demand efforts from other people without them having the opportunity to call these demands into question.

The hierarchical arrangement of issuers and receivers of instructions makes it possible, with relatively low negotiation costs (1), and relatively quickly (2), to make relatively clear decisions (3). (1): Negotiation costs are kept low by means of the fact that a hierarchical structure of organization spares cost-intensive processes of negotiation. Hierarchy liberates its participants from the necessity of engaging in complex conflicts stemming from ambiguous relationships when solving problems. The search for decisions can be abbreviated with statements such as, "Thank you for your opinion; as the supervisor, I am now deciding that we will do this in this way." (2): The speed of the decision-making process arises from the fact that managers can require their employees to assume responsibility immediately for their own choices and thereby follow management's timelines. The recipients of instructions in a hierarchy have no formal option for rejecting management's timelines. (3): Hierarchy reduces uncertainty in organizations and aims to create clarity and consistency. An organization chart developed on a hierarchical basis clearly marks who reports to whom and thereby coordinates the behavior of each recipient of instructions. If contradictions or ambiguities arise in an organization, then it is the task of the management level to impose order on the issue.

In Fordist-Taylorist organizations, management attempts to use hierarchies based on power relations to supervise new zones of uncertainty for workers. As was shown particularly clearly in the Labour Process Debate, hierarchical position enables management to mobilize and manage the growing potential of physical, human, and financial resources. Labor unions, however, often strove in vain to soften hierarchical power relations so that a "more free" power struggle was possible in the organization.

The arena in which power relations develop has changed significantly in post-bureaucratic organizations though. The resources to which stakeholders can resort in power struggles are subject to faster change. The conflict over the control of zones of uncertainty in post-bureaucratic organizations assumes a different form than is the case for Taylorist-Fordist and bureaucratic-hierarchical organizations. A diffuse, non-transparent power structure is increasingly replacing the conventional struggle for power.

Zones of Uncertainty Relevant to Power Struggles

In both traditional hierarchical and post-bureaucratic organizations, there are three additional areas, alongside the zone of uncertainty caused by hierarchy, the control of which plays an important role in internal organizational power struggles. The first area, which has central importance in the implicit and explicit power games in organizations, is the *control of environment relationships* (cf. Scott 1981). Control of environment-organization relationships is very much of fundamental importance whenever they are subjected to constant change (or through which stakeholders could be subjected to change). Taylorist-Fordist organizations pursue a strategy of sealing off the production core against possible exterior influences. One purpose of this was to ensure that production in the productive core adhered to efficient, "rational" criteria; another purpose was to take away a trump card for workers in internal organizational power struggles: control over environmental relationships. As we have seen, in post-bureaucratic organizations, it is no longer possible to separate core production and functional areas specialized in environmental relationships. This means that a worker who develops intensive relationships with a supplier, just like the employee who has personal contact with an important customer, hold important trump cards in internal organizational processes of negotiation.

The second relevant zone of uncertainty is the *control of intra-organizational communication flows*, especially the ways in which structures are formed and decisions are made. One central reason why Fordist-oriented managers view co-determination laws as an affront is the fact that at least part of their total formal control over intra-organizational processes was taken away. Faced with rising flexibility requirements, there has been increasing recognition of the fact that the complete mastery of organizational processes must be abandoned because intra-organizational information and communication flows, as well as decision-making processes, are increasingly out of management's hands. Organizational processes are increasingly escaping the formalized control of management. This development becomes particularly clear when employees in post-bureaucratic organizations even take over functions monopolized by the human resources department: decisions regarding hiring, dismissal, remuneration, and advancement. From a Marxist point of view, the power to decide about admission to and dismissal from the organization—the purchase of labor as a commodity—was particularly central for management's position of power because it thereby controlled a central zone of uncertainty. The more these central responsibilities are taken over by employees (or should be or have to be), the more the power structure of an organization shifts.

A third central resource of power is the *control of expertise*, which is expressed for example in the control of skilled competences, knowledge of work processes, or intelligence about flexible interpretations of rules in organizations. According to a thesis put forth by the Marxist organizational researcher Harry Braverman, the management strategy in Taylorist organizations consists of stripping employees of their skills by breaking down work processes, thereby controlling these zones of uncertainty (cf. Braverman 1974). This strategy aims to rob the famous figure of the maintenance worker in the tobacco industry, familiar from organizational sociology, of his central position of power. Michel Crozier visited French tobacco factories in the 1960s and discovered that the employees responsible for maintenance were the secret rulers of the company because they controlled central zones of uncertainty. Sudden machine failure was the only event that could not be predicted and was not subject generally formulated rules. The maintenance employees were the only ones who could fix this problem. No one could supervise them because nobody understood what they did (cf. Crozier 1964: 109). The efforts of a Taylorist organization sought to impose further disqualification measures so that one day this last zone of uncertainty could be taken out of the workers' hands. At the moment, however, at which a highly turbulent environment makes it necessary to bring together qualifications into the hands of individual employees, such as strategy of disqualification must fail. We find—completely in contrast to the development predicted by Braverman—that there is a strong tendency in post-bureaucratic organizations towards increasing employees' skills through job enrichment and job enlargement. Employees are supposed to master the broadest possible spectrum of activities. They are no longer paid by the work that they produce, but rather on the basis of the work that they are in a position to produce. It is only through this form of qualification that an organization can be certain that its employees are armed for any challenge that may come their way. At the same time, however, the maintenance workers in the tobacco industry go from being an exception tolerated by management to the rule.

The End of Collective Representation?

In post-bureaucratic organizations, the control of various zones of uncertainty increasingly falls to the employees. Yet this alone does not signify a fundamental redistribution of power. The power of management in Taylorist-bureaucratic organizations is only based in part on the control of individual zones of uncertainty. Management based its power primarily on a specific enchainment of controlled zones of insecurity. Only if management succeeded in extracting the necessary skills from workers and connecting these measures by means of intra- and inter-organizational processes could the influence of individual workers be minimized.

The organized labor movement, as the collective representation of workers, has a dual background: on one hand, labor unions arose from the recognition that there would be no opportunities for employees in organizations to intervene in the associative connection of individual zones of uncertainty. Only the collective organization of a broad array of work divisions could oppose the potential power of management. On the other hand, the collective bundling of employee interests enabled the channeling of conflicts in organizations. Wages were negotiated generally for all tariff workers, and conflicts were resolved in a formalized way by including the labor union. Collective representations in the work force therefore played, at least in the moderate German version, two roles in organizations: conflict regulation (bundling of protests) and relief (channeling of conflicts). This dual function of labor unions has tended to lose significance though in new forms of organization. The feeling of individual powerlessness—the point of departure for the collective organization of interests—is reduced among employees in post-bureaucratic organizations. The degree of union organization is headed towards zero in many of these organizations.

If the trends observed in post-bureaucratic organizations are to become consolidated, then there will hardly be any points of reference for the collective representation of interests in organizations. Labor unions therefore find themselves in a paradoxical situation: participation and operational co-determination, the traditional demands of labor unions, lead to a dissolution of the labor union's *raison d'être* at the very moment in which they are seriously implemented. The abolition of Taylorism, which has been one of the primary goals of labor unions for over half a century, is at the same time (one) cause for the fundamental crisis of labor unions (cf. Sainsaulieu/Segrestin 1986: 343; Knoke 2001: 295). But can employees and management in post-bureaucratic organizations manage to do without collective representation? To put it differently, does the individual worker already have sufficient individual control over zones of uncertainty? Are there new mechanisms of conflict regulation that make the channeling of conflicts superfluous?

Admittedly, individual employees in post-bureaucratic organizations often wield ever-greater control over single, discrete zones of uncertainty. The association of separate, isolated zones of uncertainty does not however take this out of the hands of management. "Executives" often have no central importance in most post-bureaucratic organizations. In some decentralized pioneering organizations, what is called "leadership as a service for the employees" seems to be management's legitimation of the control of ensembles of zones of uncertainty. Strongly decentralized organizations, for example at the software company Ploenzke, long considered one of the vanguard companies for new forms of organization, could be compared with a highway on which the employees are driving, on their own responsibility. Executives provide the infrastructure: "They run the gas stations and rest stops. They provide employees with orientation aids by enlivening the company vision each day. They are merely a helping hand that intervenes whenever there is a violation of one of the paragraphs of the 'traffic regulations'" (Fuchs 1992: 48f.).

Auto drivers, if we continue with this metaphor, have control over zones of uncertainty. They have, or at least most of them do, a license and the skills to drive a car, to communicate with other drivers in a hopefully non-aggressive and accident-free way, and to interact with their very real environment by consuming oxygen and emitting exhaust and noise. By exercising this control over different zones of uncertainty, however, they still do not have control over themselves, let alone the highway. This control rests in the hands of those who control the ensemble of zones of uncertainty. There are no signs of a revolution, or a real seizure of power by employees.

The fact that collective representation vehicles are losing significance because of the individualization of conflict regulations, accompanied simultaneously by the fact that the employee seizure of power promised by the management literature has not taken place, makes "power games" in post-bureaucratic organizations all the more complicated for everyone involved. The certainty that conflicts in organizations typically develop along the dividing line of employees (represented by the works council) and management (organizational leadership) is replaced by the uncertainty of unexplained power and conflict relationships. The dissolution of collective representation, a former central instrument for channeling conflicts, means not only that employees have lost an important protective bulwark in intra-organizational conflicts, but also that organizational leadership has to do without an important overall means of regulating organizational conflicts.

The Politicization of Everyday Life in Organizations

"The more the old system of law and order is invalidated; the more a society strives towards individuality and self-regulation—the more necessary agreements about new, self-developed rules of behavior become." This development, emphasizes Eberhard Schnelle (1989: 7), affects all areas: "The price for more individuality will be an increased willingness to engage in conflict, and more flexibility and competitiveness in terms of salary." "Increased willingness to engage in conflict," translated into the harsh reality of everyday life in organizations, means nothing other than an increase in power struggles. The dismantling of hierarchies and structures leads to a situation in which power can unfold in full bloom because it is no longer contained in hierarchies and regulated by fixed structures.

We can certainly blame hierarchy, bureaucracy, and division into departments for several pathologies in organizations. We can also complain about how much they limit the creativity and flexibility of employees. But we should not forget the role that they play in relieving strain and stress. Hierarchy, bureaucracy, and division into departments protect the weakest workers from having to constantly renegotiate their position. They reduce an organization's susceptibility to conflict because every problem, in principle, can be solved by referring to a department's competence or by sending a delegation to the next person up the chain of command. Statements such as "my department is responsible for that" or "I make this decision as your boss" may be frustrating in certain situations for those employees who are affected, but overall, hierarchies and divisional organization were and are effective mechanisms of regulating conflict from which employees can also benefit to a limited degree. What Crozier and Friedberg (1977: 92) identify for all organizations—which is in my opinion too general—will without a doubt become reality in post-bureaucratic organizations: the fact that no stable power structures exist means that all questions of power have to be fought out in more or less open conflict. In the final analysis, the organization is nothing more than a world of conflict.

Decisions based on facts become increasingly politicized in post-bureaucratic organizations. Three developments converge in this politicization. First, de-hierarchization leads to a situation in which there are no longer any structures that are clearly defined vertically or horizontally. This means in principle that anyone can criticize and call into question every decision. Influence is no longer exercised by positions, but rather—in the best case—by better arguments. Second, the standardization of the information base in organizations leads to a risk of politicization: information relevant to decision-making threatens to become ambiguous because it is exposed to an interest-laden interpretation by the stakeholders involved. Yet because the perception of information is very different due to various stakeholders because of differing "local" rationalities (Cyert/March 1963), we see again and again that decisions are made for which others also feel responsible, yet interpret the underlying information in an entirely different way. Third, constant innovations lead to an increasing politicization in post-bureaucratic organizations. Every innovation threatens to overthrow the delicate balance of power within an organization. Innovations produce new zones of uncertainty and make other zones of uncertainty less relevant. It is not said that the new zones of uncertainty are controlled by the same people who controlled the old zones of uncertainty. In this respect, the development and introduction of innovations leads increasingly to uncertainty and thereby to the politicization of the organization.

These tendencies towards politicization are often accompanied by the tabooization of power in organizations. In the self-perception of at least a few post-bureaucratic organizations, the abolition or reduction of hierarchy is synonymous with the elimination of power and power struggles. Gerard Endenburg, the long-time director of an electronics company in the Netherlands that qualified as one of the showcase companies for new forms of organization due to its so-called sociocratic approach, attributed the "power games" that still existed in his sociocratic company to the fact that his employees were influenced by an environment of autocratic decision-making structures. He hoped however that these problems would be dispelled by "win-win games" in his company. At Prométhée, a large French software applications company, decentralization and the dismantling of hierarchies led to a situation in which neither power games nor problems could be addressed openly. Prométhée developed company principles according to which every employee could perform his work autonomously while creating coordination in a friendly, non-hierarchical fashion. What at first looked like a positive corporate atmosphere, however, led to a kind of "self-censorship" (Berebbi-Hoffmann 1990: 11) in which problems and power conflicts became taboo. The internal and external demand to solve problems autonomously and to avoid endangering a good corporate environment with unnecessary tensions created an atmosphere in which communication about power relationships and key problems was no longer possible. Theoretically speaking, this was a protective reaction to the dilemma of politicization. The constant, latent danger that post-bureaucratic organizations will founder on unrestrained power struggles has the consequence that central problems and power relationships are cloaked in silence. And precisely because power and processes of power have become so central due to the dismantling of structures, they can no longer be a topic of discussion.

This process of politicization, paired with the simultaneous tabooization of power at the level of organizational sub-units, can be seen both in semi-autonomous work groups as well as project groups. The knowledge that a team failure can no longer be passed off to other departments in the organization, and the unclear definition of roles in the group and the potential for constant power struggles (cf. Reeser 1969) produce uncertainty from the perspective of the employees. This insecurity is intensified by an extreme increase in the demands placed on group members: The constant restructuring of internal work processes is often perceived as peer pressure by employees in a team. The ability of the individual to withdraw from the work process, for example by calling in sick, becomes very difficult, because this puts a burden on colleagues and not on a faceless, firmly structured organization (see also Flynn/McCombs/Elloy 1990: 27; Manz/Keating/Donnellon 1990: 21; Farrell/Morris 2013: 1376f.).

Ad hoc project groups in particular have no traditions or routines, or even formalized channels for conflict. This often leads to power struggles that are waged in subtle ways in the affected organizations. In firmly installed work groups there may be routines, but there are no formalized rules for intra-organizational cooperation and communication. Employees in work groups may no longer be exposed to anonymously formulated expectations for their position, but they do have to react instead to changing demands from their team colleagues. The main problem in early experiments with operational democracy and self-administration conducted in Sweden, Norway, and Yugoslavia in the 1970s was the lack of institutional rules for exercising power. James R. Barker, among others, noted when observing experiments with team work in U.S. companies in the 1990s that team members enforced group standards with particular zeal for sanctions (Barker 1999: 78ff.; see also Barker's earlier work in 1993). Dohse, Jürgens and Malsch even speak of the "cruelty" of team concepts in reference to experiences in the U.S. auto industry. Teams can get hold of people much harder and freeze them out much more effectively than a supervisor. But tardiness and absenteeism can also be discussed in teams. The research group saw people who "called the affected person in the morning to wake him up" (Dohse/Jürgens/Malsch 1985: 72). Due to the official justification and the confidentiality of group relationships, power however takes on a diffuse, uncontrollable character, and this is difficult to recognize or talk about.

Politicization tendencies become more severe the less group and organization members can be brought together to pursue a goal, and the less instruments are available to enlist their commitment to a centrally prescribed objective. Every form of organization is constantly endangered by the limited rationality of its members' behavior. Restricted or bounded rationality, a term that originated with the economist Herbert A. Simon, points to the fact that organization members are not in a position to orient themselves towards an all-encompassing rationality. Instead they develop local logics of action that are adapted to the state of their knowledge and consciousness. Furthermore, the members of an organization always have their own free space, which they seek to defend and expand. This constantly raises the danger that they will undermine organizational connections. Furthermore, the legitimacy of organizational goals are constantly weakened and questioned by the interests, goals, and values of the organization's members.

In post-bureaucratic organizations, this problem becomes worse because decentralization and profit centers, as well as the emphasis on individuality and autonomy of employees, favors the formation of local, bounded rationalities. At the same time, proven methods are no longer available to channel the bounded rationalities of organization members towards the organization's objective. This is why we are often dealing with an extreme form of problem-solving in post-bureaucratic organizations: the interests and rationalities of the individual organization members are strongly differentiated. There is no fixed arena for waging conflicts, and stakeholders can threaten to outsource decisions based on their qualifications and their exterior relationships. In contrast to constellations in which there is a safe consensus about collective goal-setting and cooperation rules can be reached, or at least a "consensus can be fabricated" in the context of process rules (cf. Burawoy 1979), there are hardly any recognized rules of the game in highly politicized organizations, and the conflict frequently covers up the definition of the problem.

This "differentiation based on politicization" has frequently taken place in political organizations, where different substantive positions often legitimate merely personal animosities. Such processes of differentiation are only possible in organizations, however, if the politicization processes furthered by de-hierarchization cannot be contained by the organization. Henry Mintzberg illustrates the dangers of post-bureaucratic organizations in an impressive way: "No structure is more Darwinist, none requires more of the fit—so long as they remain fit—and none is more devastating for the weak. Fluid structures encourage internal competition and are sometimes fertile soil for major power struggles. The French have an evocative description of these kinds of processes: *un panier du crabes*, or a basket full of crabs; they are all pinching each other to work their way up higher, or even to get out" (1979: 462).

4.3 The Complexity Dilemma: Simplification Strategies That Make Things More Complicated

British Petroleum (BP) was certainly never suspected in the past of being a post-bureaucratic company par excellence; BP was typically compared more to a heavy battleship from the 1950s rather than the flexible, maneuverable fleet of the early twenty-first century. This was supposed to change, at least according to BP's CEO Robert Horton in the 1990s. He promoted the reduction of complexity throughout the entire corporation: less bureaucracy and hierarchy, a "slim" and adaptable headquarters, and action-oriented teams that connected with each other as in a network. Decision-making paths were supposed to be simplified, responsibility situated in the future with individuals and no longer with the previously ubiquitous "committees." The latter, as well as the supervisory management levels, were also to be replaced to a large extent. If we are to believe Robert Horton, then BP in the 1990s was moving towards the resolution of internal organizational "complexity, bureaucracy, and uncertainty" to focus in the future on "simplicity, team work, and trust" (Horton 1990: 27).

What BP was alluding to—the ostensible goodbye to complexity—is also propounded as an objective among post-bureaucratic organizations. Despite fundamental differences in their form of organization, traditional and post-bureaucratic organizations agree on one thing: an enormous dread of being destroyed by too much complexity. Whether post-bureaucratic or not, growing internal and external turbulence are perceived by individual employees as increasing, sometimes almost unbearable complexity. Managers feel overwhelmed by a flood of information and rapid changes. In traditional organizations, "simple" employees take refuge from growing pressures and contradictory demands by embracing the deceptive hope that "the higher-ups" already have everything under control. They hang on to this illusion that somebody at the top must be able to exercise mastery of this rich, detailed complexity. But it is precisely the people at the top that feel overwhelmed by these complex situations. Their consultants—first and foremost McKinsey—even view "overcomplexity" as a "mortal danger" for organizations (Roever 1991).

The terms "complexity driver" and "overcomplexity" have become management's worst nightmares in recent years. Organizational consultants of all stripes recommend doing away with this organizational-structural monster as quickly as possible. The points of attack seem familiar: overly complex production processes, to much product diversity, value creation chains that are too long, and overly strong centralization. Organizations are urged to conduct simplification campaigns to liberate themselves from the most prominent "complexity drivers"—an organization structured to a high degree along the lines of division of labor, an overly extensive product portfolio, and excessive automation. The same managers and scholars who were still preaching the expansion of service offerings a few years ago to generate synergy effects and provide a hedge against market turbulence now call for trimming down over-complex, cumbersome organizations.

Lean Management—The Futile Struggle Against Complexity

If we are to believe leading international consulting firms, then one of the main challenges for organizations in the twenty-first century is to offer customers an optimal service while simultaneously becoming a gigantic, highly complex organization. In order to make their own customers aware of the problem of "overcomplexity," consultants from the major classical corporate consulting firms even invented a new cost factor in organizations: "complexity costs." Depending on the number of products, the portfolio of tasks, production flows, and the type of warehousing, the complexity costs stood somewhere between 10 and 40 percent of total costs (Child et al. 1991: 73). "Complexity problems" were identified at all of the companies that used raw materials and packaging primarily for just one product, had large storage facilities, needed lots of time for product development, worked with several independent information systems, were structured in isolated functional groups, and consisted of more than five hierarchical levels.

Management consultants recommended therapies that were called "complexity optimization," "right-sizing," or "reengineering" to gain control over the complexity costs that they had identified. With these hollow words, they extolled everything that guaranteed them the attention of European and North American managers: dismantling hierarchies would shorten decision-making paths. Company process that were critical to success are "accelerated to the max" in the context of "turbo-marketing" and "high-speed management." Center concepts enable the removal of fixed-cost blocks and increase awareness of costs and revenue. Instead of getting bogged down, people concentrated on core competences and key products. Production depth was reduced by means of outsourcing. These simplifications streamlined and accelerated companies, making them successful (cf. Rommel/Brück/Diederichs 1993).

Decades after its invention, Lean Management is still in many places praised as an effective and efficient lever for reducing complexity. Even if the concept has been renamed many times in the interim so that it would not be associated with the high number of failed Lean Management products, streamlining work processes seems for many managers to still be one of the most seductive methods of attaining fitness. The overall strategy of Lean Management strives towards the systematic dismantling of hedging measures (buffers) while simultaneously implementing robust, simple solutions with high process certainty. Lean Management is perfectionist in its basic conception and anticipates—just like bureaucracies, incidentally—preventive care for all conceivable cases.

Reducing the diversity of parts and outsourcing production steps is meant to reduce internal organizational complexity. Formerly internal operational functions are farmed out external service providers and suppliers under the catchword of outsourcing. Less is done in-house, and more is purchased. This is meant to redirect complexity problems, such as constantly changing technology, personnel scarcity, and training, outside of the company. The company concentrates on its core business, where it expects the highest "return on investment." The actual product is assembled in a modular way. The modules are prefabricated by system suppliers and delivered just in time.

Zero-error requirements for suppliers and employees, and the imposition of constant improvement processes, are meant to perfect logistics and the production process. The responsibility for this perfection is no longer outsourced from direct production, as in Taylorism, but rather is integrated with the involvement of all employees and suppliers in the production process. The "Kaizen" of employees is a highly standardized and formalized process. Improvements can only be initiated within the framework of clearly prescribed procedures. The power for making decisions about organizational changes remains with the managers.

Inside of organizations, information paths are shortened, processes simplified, and clear targets are pressed into the hands of every employee. People reduce the number of hierarchy levels without doing away with the organizational principle of hierarchy. Only the chains of command and instruction are streamlined. Teamwork can also be integrated into this hierarchical organization concept.

Lean Production does not do away with automation and technology. However, people strive for the automation of simple production processes, not complicated work steps. Due to this self-limitation in the subject of automation, the required machines can be produced in a company's own manufacturing plant instead of having to be purchased from external providers. People try with this strategy to reduce complexity in the areas of fully automated production.

If we take the classical expert consulting firms at their word, then Lean Management is a promising battle cry against complexity in organizations. While Taylorism and bureaucracies, with their high degree of division of labor, are damned as complexity drivers (Child et al. 1991: 78), some believe that it is possible to fight "overcomplexity" with streamlining and slimming regimes. The simplifying opposition of Lean Management as an urgently needed streamlining strategy, and Taylorism as an outmoded, complexity-driving mode of production, is questionable at first glance; indeed, Taylor himself strove for the simplification of industrial production with his scientific management method. The scientific planning and precise calculations of every workstation was meant to reduce complexity in production, not increase it. Even if the entire organization, with its different workstations, seems highly complex at first, these work positions and their connections were nevertheless precisely defined.

Even in the practice of Taylorist production, it is possible to see that the streamlining of complexity is a general strategy. The precision, consistency, discipline, tightness, and reliability of Taylorist or bureaucratically structured organizations is supposed to guarantee that a properly prepared solution was on hand for every possible problem. The breakdown, standardization and formalization of processes had one goal: to guarantee efficient production flows or—to put it differently—to reduce the complexity of organized economic activity to a minimum. In bureaucratic and Taylorist organizations, we have to deal with the paradox that, although management strategy aims at a reduction of complexity, the result however—and here McKinsey and the like are correct—leads to the emergence of highly complex production processes. The reduction of every employee's scope of work leads to lower motivation and greater tolerance for production errors— and thereby to increased complexity. Whoever wants to reduce the complexity of up- and downstream production steps by means of own production must always master ever more comprehensive processes in their totality. The simplification strategy of subdividing into functional areas leads to an increase in the need for coordination among the functionally defined departments. The separation of value creation and development, conceived of as a reduction in complexity, ends in highly complex and slow innovation processes.

What then allows us now to assume that Lean Management does not follow the same diabolical development as Taylorism? In view of the contradiction between Taylorist target-setting and the result that finally comes about as a result of it, it is necessary to take a more nuanced view of Taylorism as a complexity driver and to transfer experiences to post-bureaucratic organizations in general and Lean Management in particular. The same dilemma that faces Taylorism threatens Lean Management, which is designed as a simplification strategy along the lines of Taylorism: the reduction of complexity, which is in the final analysis nothing other than a surreptitious increase in complexity.

The outsourcing of production areas only promises a simplification of organizational structure at first glance. Outsourcing strategies often end in a shift of complexity, not in its reduction. Complexity is moved from purely internal organizational areas to departments that are responsible for environment relationships. Outsourcing leads to significant rises in the need to coordinate between the organization and supplier firms: the more resolute the principle of outsourcing is followed, the higher the requirements will be for managing the interface to the exterior market. People don't have to bother with in-house

IT people anymore; now they have to deal with expensive ones from the outside.

Lean concepts envision organizing relationships between companies and suppliers in a fragile way so that materials can be delivered just before the time at which it is needed in production. Although this may enable reductions in warehousing costs, or at least pushing them off to suppliers, general logistics then becomes extremely susceptible to disruptions. The absence of materials, or defective materials, can bring production to a standstill. This is why just-in-time concepts require intensive maintenance and quality assurance efforts, as well as changed supplier-purchaser relationships. Despite all of the logic surrounding the simplification of complexity, both scenarios—the frequent occurrence of disruptions and the intensification of relationships to suppliers—lead to an increase in complexity, not a reduction.

This "fragile lean" logic is also applied within organizations. There are no reserves for breakdowns in the production process, regardless of what may cause them. Every assembly-line worker can or should stop the conveyor belt if he sees a defect in a product. This process, just like the fragile organization of supplier-purchaser relationships, is also risky and extremely complex.

The tight staffing in Lean Management organizations is meant to streamline the organization and reduce complexity. If however the organization does not want to run the danger of suffering staff shortages in certain critical situations, then flexibility must be assured by placing increased demands on employees. This does not reduce complexity; it hides it. Coping with this complexity is shoved off on to the employees, whose activities intensify and who also work overtime when they are overloaded. The fact that overtime hours and capacity overload lead to a higher frequency of errors and increased risks in production can be seen already in Taylorist organizations.

The discussion surrounding Lean Management has won over completely new adherents to the idea of team concepts as a rationalization strategy. The fact that the introduction of teams is being sold as a method of simplifying organizations is puzzling; production by teams comprised of interdisciplinary members are typically much more complex than production that is broken down into its smallest functional pieces. In the latter case, everything is defined precisely; in the former, everything is basically open to change.

The discussion about the problems of Lean Management has overlooked the fact that it is precisely in Lean Management organizations that high complexity surfaces; this form of organization is a complexity driver in the truest sense of the word. People reduce the discussion to the idea that the objective may be simplification, yet the way to get there is unfortunately complex, and employees unfortunately do not have the necessary competences yet. So management magazines proclaimed monotonously that slimming-down regimes may limit complexity, but the path to reduced-complexity organizations is unfortunately highly complex. In the svelte paradise of Lean Production, management's life is easier because of reduced complexity, although the road to get there costs "blood, sweat and tears." The causes for this highly complex change process is claimed to be incapable or insufficiently trained staff. Every employee was identified as a potential stumbling block on the way to the streamlined organization: production employees were accused of lacking team spirit and the ability to work in teams. They resisted the intensification of their work and efforts to make it more flexible. The relationship between employees and employers suffered under rationalization efforts. Middle management retreated into a mental bunker of denial in the face of fears about dismantling levels of hierarchy. Suppliers felt bossed around by the new terms of the end manufacturers, and last but not least, top management lacked sufficient knowledge about Lean Production.

Explaining the failure of an organizational strategy as the result of the impotence of managers and employees is not just unsatisfactory in intellectual terms; it also keeps a management ready for change from seeing the structural problems of new organizational concepts. This is why we have to look beyond personalized identifications of problems to the analysis of streamlining concepts, whether under the original name of Lean Management or one of its renamed derivatives. Instead, we ought to address the unfounded hope of organizations that a strategy of complexity simplification truly does simplify complexity.

Complexity Reduction That Creates New Complexity

Whether complexity reducers along the lines of McKinsey or devotees of Lean Management, all of them assume that simple rules and simple structures also lead to simple, low-complexity organizations. Recent findings in mathematics, economics, physics, and biology all demonstrate how illusory this assumption really is. An interdisciplinary research group in Santa Fe, New Mexico, founded in the 1980s, has repeatedly encountered the phenomenon that simple rules create highly complex systems. For example, they have shown that simple calculation rules, when applied repeatedly, create complex, self-similar structures. Using the calculation rule $z(n+1) = [z(n)^2] + c$ results in complex series of numbers, called fractals, which exhibit structures that are similar, yet never completely the same (cf. Mandelbrot 1983, for example). In order to explain this principle, which also occurs in chemistry, astronomy, and economics, John H. Holland, a scholar at the Santa Fe Institute, points to games that generate highly complex game play with just a few rules. Although (or better: because) chess has such a low number of rules, it became such a complicated game that even grandmasters and powerful computers can only begin to comprehend its complexity (cf. Waldrop 1992: 151f.). The economist William Brian Arthur explains the phenomenon in an even more striking way: allow a drop of water to fall on a smooth surface. A complex droplet structure forms, not because there are highly complicated rules governing this action, but because two relatively simple rules mutually supplement one another: on one hand, gravity tries to drive the water apart and cover the surface with a thin, flat film of water. On the other hand, the surface tension of water molecules drives them to come together and join into a large, compact ball. The mix of these two simple rules produces does not just produce complex droplet patterns; in fact, every pattern is unique. If we repeat the experiment, a fully new arrangement occurs (cf. Waldrop 1992: 36).

Management's desperate struggle against overcomplexity and complexity drivers is directed against the same phenomenon that makes chess such a highly complex game and that bring water to form a bizarre, unique pattern on a surface: complexity arises through the interplay of a few simple rules; it is not the result of a comprehensive, detailed body of rules. The development of both Taylorism and Lean Management show that, when faced with an increasingly complex environment, all attempts at reducing complexity are, in the final analysis, futile. Every reduction in complexity leads to new, increased complexity.

In specific terms, this means that management, overwhelmed as they are by proliferating organizational structures, growing product portfolios, and lengthy decision-making procedures, is pursuing traditional objectives—whether we call it slimming down or streamlining—that ultimately lead to increased complexity: "Every simplification increases complexity, a complexity that doesn't crop up just anywhere, but rather precisely at the point where the simplification was carried out … Simplicity is not the antonym of complexity; instead, it is a moment of overcoming complexity that contributes to the increase of complexity" (Baecker 1992: 56). Simplicity is therefore not the classical opposite of complexity, despite what McKinsey and our everyday understanding may suggest. Organizations do not face an alternative between a strategy that increases complexity and one that simplifies it. An organization is neither highly complex nor simple; instead, it can increase its complexity through simplification strategies.

If we suspend the classical opposition of simplification and complication, it becomes comprehensible why Lean Management, like all other complexity reduction concepts, rests on fundamentally questionable premises. The removal of time buffers as a rationalization strategy leads to increased susceptibility to failure. Kaizen as a continual improvement concept results in the loss of all flexibility. Perfecting production processes leads again to increased complexity.

The complexity dilemma for post-bureaucratic organizations lies in the fact that employees, facing complexity and confusion inside and outside the organization, long for simple, slim, complexity-reducing structures, although these structures would then lead to an additional increase in confusion. It is a small comfort to post-bureaucratic organizations that even highly bureaucratized organizations strive to reduce complexity. Even employees of companies, administrations, hospitals, universities and schools, who have persevered through years of organizational numbness, still strive for simplicity and certainty. This should give members of post-bureaucratic organizations a taste of what is to come in terms of overcoming complexity. The more turbulent the environment, the more unstable the paths for communication and decision-making become; and the more open and therefore complex internal processes area, the stronger and more understandable efforts for clear and simple structures and processes are. Post-bureaucratic organizations are ultimately the organizational reaction to major environmental turbulence. They can only gain control of this chaos because they adjust their complex internal processes to this exterior world. Post-bureaucratic organizations, despite their thirst for simple structures, are damned to be complex.

Complexity is brought into post-bureaucratic organizations in diverse ways. Organizations have two options for confronting this. In the course of a comprehensive functional integration, they can integrate the purchasing, planning, development, and sales divisions into the production division. The alternative is to have decentralized organizational units use the shared resources of the entire organization. Both cases result in an increase in complexity. In the first case, complexity issues from the fact that redundant functions would be set up in the various autonomous units. Each autonomous unit would now have its own purchasing, development and sales functions. New and complex cooperative relationships would have to be built up to derive synergy effects from these decentralized functions. In the second case, complexity lies in the access that decentralized organizational units have to centralized resources. Complicated processes of negotiation emerge if various autonomous units access centrally organized sales or purchasing functions.

The dilemma no longer lies in the notion that these measures lead to an increase in complexity rather than the yearned-for reduction in complexity; instead, the real dilemma is the incapacity of those involved to perceive this phenomenon for what it is. The run on simplification and streamlining strategies in management conceals risks, even "mortal dangers": the increasing complexity is not perceived because people are counting on a reduction. The organization is no longer able to handle the complexity that comes as a consequence of simplification strategies. Forced simplifications contradict the inherent laws of systems. The system "defends itself" and develops a complexity that management can no longer control.

Help promises a change in perception: organizations have to understand complexity as a challenge, not as a mortal danger. Due to rapidly changing market conditions and technological upheavals, an organization cannot harbor hopes that environmental conditions will be simple, clearly structured, and steady. Organizations can only meet the demands of a complex environment if they manage to adjust to this by means of internal organizational complexity.

We need fewer "heroes of chaos" or "masters of complexity" and more open, flexible organizational structures that predetermine as few reactions as possible. For organizations, this means resisting the pressure to organize production processes into lean forms. It means viewing unpredictability as something positive, to be understood as innovation potential, and not to perfect organizations but to design them to be error-friendly. What we need is to face up to new, complex environmental conditions and to say our final goodbyes to chimerical hopes for simple, lean structures.

5.
Beyond Hierarchy and Anarchy

To know and note the living, you'll find it
Best to first dispense with the spirit:
Then with the pieces in your hand,
Ah! You've only lost the spiritual bond.
Johann Wolfgang von Goethe [Faust I, lines 1936-1939]

The dilemmas of identity, politicization, and complexity are three fundamental challenges for post-bureaucratic organizations, and the responses to them have proven up to now to be inadequate. Organizations face a precarious situation in which the necessary development of self-organizing partially autonomous units makes the integration of these units increasingly difficult, yet also ever more essential. As they have shifted their direction to increasingly autonomous units, organizations have dismantled many interfaces, indirect routes, and redundancies in communication and cooperation. At the same time, however, increasing mutual dependencies in decentralized organizations have created new cooperation needs that have to be satisfied.

Given this unsettled situation, it seems that there is a powerful temptation for organizations to respond to emerging problems of identity, politicization, and complexity with proven concepts of stabilization. Thus, a once-pioneering operation of Mercedes Benz that had done away with very fast speed specifications in an assembly line returned to extremely short unit cycles in assembly line production. ABB, which for a long time was a role model for other companies due to its largely independent elements, gave the command to retreat years ago: instead of decentralization with broad autonomy for the business units, a few functions were again centralized under the label of "integrative decentralization." In other companies, the improved economic situation, and the concomitant increase in orders, led to the undoing of painstakingly implemented group work because it proved difficult to integrate part-time workers who were hired on a short-term basis into the groups. Other companies who had outsourced purchasing to the decentralized company units were exposed to the temptation to bring purchasing back into the staff that reports to the management board, because of ostensible cost advantages.

These attempts at "recentralization," which follow every wave of decentralization, are understandable as a reaction to the diverse problems of organizations that are oriented towards flexibility. They probably also make sense in individual cases, yet they do not constitute a generally applicable strategy due to growing flexibility requirements. Returning to traditional hierarchical and centralized structures—at least in the eyes of most organizations—does not seem to solve the core problem of organizations.

In view of growing flexibility requirements and increasingly free power games, the challenge for organizations seems to lie in finding new and appropriate means to integrate employees toward the achievement of an organizational goal. In the face of the threat of organizational dispersion, the blurring of boundaries with the exterior world, and increasing internal politicization, an organization's success depends increasingly on attaining a high degree of integration and stability.

Even traditional organizational consulting firms seem to have realized that conventional management instruments, in the form of "management by concepts," fail when they run up against flexibility requirements. Even the dinosaurs of the expert consulting industry, which have left their imprimatur across the international organizational landscape after decades of standard products and patented solutions, see that they are approaching their conceptual limits. The "new insecurity" or "new complexity" resulting from flexibility requirements and power structures that are becoming ever more complex, forces post-bureaucratic organizations to adopt structures that usher in the necessary stabilization and integration. These structures however cannot be maneuvers for falling back again to the old proven stabilization mechanisms, such as hierarchy, centralization, or sealing off from the exterior world.

Given the various possible ways in which post-bureaucratic organizations can develop, statements about how organizations should deal with growing problems of identity, politicization, and complexity necessarily have a merely speculative character. In this chapter, I show how management principles can be based on recent findings in complexity and chaos research, and developed beyond the dichotomy of hierarchy and anarchy. From a social sciences perspective, using the scientific findings of complexity and chaos research is not without its problems. Organizations, as social systems, are subject to their own autonomous laws, which can only be changed in very limited ways by means of knowledge about scientific research on complexity and chaos. Connections to research on complexity and chaos can therefore only be understood as propositions and speculations that can improve our comprehension of which direction our responses to identity, politicization, and complexity problems should take.

I show that the management literature assumes that the self-organization of decentralized units can only thrive in a condition of unlimited instability, meaning a state in which neither inflexibility nor explosive chaos has the upper hand (Section 5.1). This kind of management locates "stabilization concepts" of post-bureaucratic organizations, such as exercising influence by specifying contexts, beyond the realm of order and chaos. These concepts appear to be a first response—even if it is an unsatisfactory answer—to the dilemmas of identity, politicization, and complexity (Section 5.2). From an organizational science perspective, it is naive to assume that binding principles have already emerged for the management of post-bureaucratic organizations. What appears to be necessary is not new panaceas, but instead a deeper understanding of how organizations function that goes beyond bureaucracy and hierarchy (Section 5.3).

5.1 Can We Escape the Dilemma?
Management at the Edge of Chaos

"In a communication society with a service culture," says management consultant Jürgen Fuchs, "we can no longer reduce complexity and make it manageable by means of breaking things down and bureaucratization." He believes that the only solution "is the targeted increase of complexity in specialized, autonomous, and transparent units" (Fuchs 1992: 48). In its convoluted way, this observation contains one of the central ideas for the organization of post-bureaucratic organizations: it is neither about change as the only constant, nor about the reduction of complexity, which is futile anyway. What is called for is the targeted increase of complexity and a simultaneous rise in transparency. As the organizational psychologist Karl Weick (1976) recognized, this is about the skillful combination of loose connections in organizations, which enables flexibility, with fixed connections that generate stability.

The regular debacles of long-term planning show that organizations in the twenty-first century have suffered from too little internal complexity and insecurity, not too much. Managers and employees appear to have separated themselves from a long-popular assumption, namely that insecurity and instability are the consequences of incompetence and ignorance. These uncertainties however are now increasingly understood as a necessary, even vital, foundation for the organizations of the twenty-first century. Of course, complexity, chaos, and instability destroy everyday routines in an organization; routines that often guarantee a significant share of value creation. Yet the management literature claims that it is precisely this process of creative destruction that creates space for innovation and change. The dangers of insecurity and instability are thereby transformed into opportunities for surprise. Chaos, to put it briefly, becomes an "invitation to adventure."

In order for the process of destruction to be creative and not ruinous, for uncertainty and complexity not to attain explosive, threatening dimensions, but remain useable in a productive way by organizations, then people in organizations seem to strive to limit chaos through organizational means. According to this view, organizations have to increase their internal complexity, yet use streamlined, decentralized structures to make it possible to control complexity. In systems theory terminology, this is about an increase in internal complexity with synchronously integrated, ever more refined "complexity simplification matrices." Thus Gerard Endenburg (1986: 6), one of the promoters of the "dynamic-cyclical sociocratic model," emphasizes that organizations have to make "both/and" decisions, not "either/or": both hierarchy and equality; organizational control both through employees and management; both creative chaos and certainty—and we could add: stability as well as flexibility and change.

Organizations apparently have to confront with increasing frequency contrasting, paradoxical demands: They see the compulsion to simultaneously increase and reduce their complexity. They have to dis-integrate, and they have to integrate at the same time. They have to be global actors while also having local roots. They have to organize creative chaos as well as order, and they have to be flexible and stable. There is a view that is increasingly predominant, namely that dealing with dilemmas, ambiguity, and contradictions is becoming a decisive factor for the success of organizations.

The challenge for organizations seems to lie in finding a balance that allows both sides of a dilemma to operate at the same time. The two poles, which are actually contradictory, have to be capable of unfolding at the same time in organizations, according to the view in management. Post-bureaucratic organizations can only retain and improve their performance by means of this new mixture of mechanisms of flexibility and stability. Only the simultaneous double reference to repetition and change elevates post-bureaucratic organizations to a level at which flexibility requirements and process integration become compatible with one another. It is not a one-sided emphasis on the ability to change, but rather an intelligent mix of routines, rituals, and programs with an opening of the organization towards change that make it possible to productively implement external chaos without faltering on excessive internal uncertainty.

What should this kind of strategy look like? What inspires it? The meteorologist and chaos researcher Edward N. Lorenz noted as early as the 1960s that small changes can have major effects down the line. Lorenz found that a tiny deviation in initial conditions can have a fundamental influence on the development of the entire system. This was the discovery of what is called the butterfly effect. The beat of a butterfly's wing in Japan can amplify positive and negative feedback loops in a weather system in such a way that it unleashes a hurricane in Arkansas. Using mosquito swarms, computer programs, and futures contracts on the commodities markets, scientists demonstrated how chaotic systems cope with uncertainty and rapid change. Even if we only have a vague idea of the direction in which chaotic or complex systems develop, and forecasts about their future lie largely outside of our range, we can still recognize very specific principles that govern their functioning (cf. Valery 1989).

In view of the regulatory mechanisms in chaotic systems, there is no longer a reason to be afraid of chaos, according to the tenor in the management literature: It is apparent that order does not always descend into chaos, but that the opposite also happens: chaos has a hidden order. Chaos today describes both exceptional states and normality. As the shoe manufacturer Think says, chaos typically triumphs over order because chaos is simply better organized. For organizations that want to be open to uncertainty and instability, it depends on using the highly complex patterns of order that are concealed within chaos, without being drawn into an uncontrollable, highly explosive situation. What we need are not "organizations of chaos," but rather "organizations on the edge of chaos": organizations that manage to find purchase in the constantly shifting "battleground" between stagnation and anarchy (cf. Ruthen 1993: 138).

Organizations in the Realm of Limited Instability

The chaos researcher Ralph D. Stacey (1992: 63ff.) described years ago what a system that exists beyond a state of stagnation or anarchy would look like. He proposes that organizations be organized according to the model of systems that occupy a space of "limited instability." This means being inspired by systems that have already exited the state of stable balance, yet have not flipped over into the stage of explosive chaos. In a phase of limited instability, systems can develop highly complex behaviors. For example, if a heated gas is in a state of thermodynamic balance, then the atoms emanate a non-directed, diffuse light. The gas behaves like a normal lamp with a range of a few meters. If we continue heating the gas, however, the gas leaves the state of balance and the atoms fly wildly about each other. Their behavior becomes chaotic. In this state of instability, the atoms reach a critical point at which they suddenly begin to organize themselves. All of the atoms together throw a directed, bundled beam of light. The result of this highly complex behavior in the state of limited instability is a laser, a coherent beam of light that can extend over very great distances (cf. Stacey 1992: 63ff.).

In the field of limited instability, the long-term developments of a system are random; however, they are random within the framework of predictable boundaries. Stacey (1992: 63) observes that stable feedback rules culminate in complex processes that can no longer be directly derived from these rules. Thus, the weather system is driven by non-linear feedback loops. Self-amplifying circles of storms, low- and high-pressure areas, heat waves and cold snaps, make long-term weather predictions impossible. Meteorologists can only predict tomorrow's weather with some degree of certainty. But even if they cannot make specific predictions about the weather in three weeks' time, we know that it will always be similar to the weather than we normally have around this time of year. We know that weather patterns are limited in such a way that only certain variants can develop. Before holes in the ozone layer and the greenhouse effect made us horribly aware of the complexity of the earth's systems, we could still presume, with a probability bordering on certainty, that we will not experience heat waves in the Arctic, and that we are safe from snowstorms in the Sahara.

Organizations are forced to deal with the very limited predictability of complex systems on a day-to-day basis. In the process, though, they do not have to have the same negative experience as the video system developer Beta. In the mid-1970s, VHS and Beta fought for dominance on the video recorder market—a market that today no longer plays a role because of the Internet. Experts found that the Beta system was technically superior to the VHS system. Electronics manufacturers, who would have used this information to make predictions for the future, would still be sitting on their Beta video recorders without the slightest chance of arousing one ounce of interest among customers for their products. What had happened? The sellers of the VHS system had the good fortune of having a minimal jump on the market when they started selling their product, despite the technical disadvantages of their system. Because electronics stores did not want to offer two different kinds of devices for the same purpose and wanted to push customers toward a uniform system, there was a strong tendency to buy the market leader's devices. VHS' minimal lead was enough to make it the only system on the market for video recorders within a few years. The Beta system completely disappeared, despite its technical advantages (cf. Waldrop 1992: 36).

The same effect that led the Beta video system to retreat into oblivion also led to the form of today's typewriter and computer keyboards. The QWERTY layout, named after the first six letters on the uppermost line of U.S. keyboards, dominates the design of typewriters and computers, with minimal modifications, in the entire Western world. But the QWERTY model that tortures all of us to greater or lesser degrees today is definitely not the most efficient and user-friendly system. It was developed by the engineer Christopher Scholes in 1873 to slow down the typing speed of secretaries. The type levers of the typewriters at the time would jam if the operator was typing too fast. When the Remington Sewing Machine Company mass-produced typewriters with QWERTY keyboards and brought them to market, ever more typists adopted this system. Other typewriter manufacturers were therefore forced to adapt to the QWERTY model. Eventually, the other models that had allowed faster typing speeds disappeared from the market, and so today—and likely for all time—QWERTY became part of Western typing culture (cf. David 1986), although in the meantime the technical options for a more effective system are available. If a typewriter manufacturer at the end of the nineteenth century had insisted on producing a more effective model, thereby ignoring the possibility that small details can have big consequences, then that firm would have fallen victim to its belief in the best technical solution. Organizational leaders can learn just how futile long-term planning is by looking at QWERTY, Beta, and VHS. The only thing that planning-obsessed managers can assume with near certainty is that their long-term plans will not come to fruition. There is not just one predictable future for an organization; there are several possible futures. The future that emerges depends on small details, the developments of which are not predictable. The desire to determine an organization's future in advance would be equivalent to Don Quixote tilting at the windmills of complexity.

Systems in the borderland between chaos and stable balance— whether for weather, post-bureaucratic organizations, mosquito swarms, or gas entities—have irregular patterns and are not completely random. Previously existing stagnation and stability may dissolve in the transition to limited instability, yet the system retains its coherence by means of abstract patterns. Let's look at one example that chaos researchers often refer to: We can assume that when rain meets freezing temperatures, snowflakes will form. Yet we cannot determine the precise form of the flake. Even if every single snowflake is clearly a snowflake, they are all different. Every snowflake is the result of its specific history of getting to the earth: what kind of cloud it came from, to what temperature swings and air pressure changes it was subjected, how closely it fell to other snowflakes. As observers, we only see the "snowflake" pattern, and a detailed definition would be an impossible undertaking (cf. Stacey 1992: 67).

Patterns are a particular organization of elements that cannot be explained in detail. Although they are irregular in their individual behavior, the elements compose themselves in agreement with the overall structure of the system. The formation of patterns contains the expectation that elements will arrange themselves within a roughly defined structure, although it depends on each individual case as to how this order will emerge in relation to a specific situation. The idea of the pattern enables the unification of the two central aspects of post-bureaucratic organizations: it refers on one hand to the existing opportunity to do justice to change. The ways in which order forms within a superordinate structure remains open. Communication can flow freely. Coordination structures can form flexibly as long as everything remains in the framework of the overall structure. On the other hand, the idea of the pattern refers to the fact that there is something like a superordinate stability, a rough framework for orientation. This therefore fulfills the requirement that even a highly flexible, highly innovative organization must have at least a modicum of structure (cf. Crozier/Friedberg 1977: 406).

What does pattern formation then look like in the specific practices of the business world? Ralph D. Stacey notes that high-tech companies set up shop around certain highly innovative research institutes. The proximity to research centers in Stanford and Berkeley played an important role in the rise of Silicon Valley in California. In a similar way, a research institute in Cambridge in England attracted an entire network of electronics and information technology companies. Dense research landscapes, such as in the area between Reading and Bristol in Great Britain, or along Boston's Route 128, led to the development of completely new branches of industry. We can observe a certain pattern of economic development here. We cannot understand, however, the specific forms. We do note however that research centers can have a positive influence on regional economic development. Why, when, and how companies hook up with these centers, or decide move to a specific place, lies beyond our understanding (cf. Stacey 1992: 68). The desperate and often futile attempts by governments to attract high-tech firms to settle down in their cities demonstrates how difficult it is to imitate the Silicon Valley pattern. The empty technology centers in many cities are the result of unsuccessful attempts to use detailed economic development plants to copy patterns that are the result of the complex escalation of a few small influencing factors.

The stock market is also an example of how patterns emerge in a state of limited instability. Price developments in the financial markets obviously cannot be predicted. Otherwise, all brokers would have become wealthier in the meantime than they already area, and market speculators wouldn't be able to make a name for themselves because speculation cannot take place under conditions of forecasting certainty. Yet despite the fact that every single price change occurs randomly, there are pattern formations. The founder of fractal geometry, Benoît Mandelbrot, fed cotton prices for the last sixty years into a large computer. There were strange symmetries in the daily, monthly, and annual price developments. The hidden patterns found by Mandelbrot proved that even in such complex systems as stock exchanges, patterns arise that can be understood by people (cf. Mandelbrot 1989).

Increasing numbers of organizations are profiting from limited instability and surprising pattern formations. Organizational consultants have observed that many organizations are in a constant back and forth between centralization and decentralization. As if they were caught between two magnets, organizations are pulled back and forth between a state of stable, centralized balance and a diffuse, decentralized imbalance. However, only at the first glance does it seem that organizations are looking for the perfect state between centralization and decentralization. Instead, organizations profit from the fact that they are in a process of change, of limited instability. In this framework, irregular patterns and regulation mechanisms can arise that are attributable neither to purely centralized nor decentralized strategy.

Self-organization

If we confront someone with clear definitions and structures, he will behave in such a way that nothing remains clear and structured. Almost every authoritarian father, every patriarchal business leader, and every autocrat has already had this experience. There is however a counter-process that combats this tendency to destroy rigid orders: If we confront a person with instability, states that appear surprisingly and then disappear, with intelligent antagonisms and deficient communication, then this person will begin to define goals and form his own structures and certainties. To put it differently, if we grant freedom and self-determination, then people will organize themselves. If we mandate a firmly defined purpose and a prescribed objective, then people will look around for something else. The benefit of unpredictability, uncertainty, and complexity is that people who face the chaos of seeming randomness are forced to create their own structures and clarity. Self-organization can develop.

In many companies, administrations, armies, hospitals, and universities, self-organization has become a magic word.[19] Every instance of "management by objectives"—employees performing a clearly prescribed task on their own—is sold as a self-organizing process. Every small expansion in the spectrum of tasks and responsibilities elevates a team to a self-organizing group. The fact that self-organization means that employees assume responsibility for all of the processes—from defining the goal to post-attainment review—is often quickly forgotten, or completely ignored, in the euphoria over self-management. People rarely think enough about the prerequisites and conditions that can facilitate the development of self-organization. A few veterans among the business leaders, for example, do not see the problem with dovetailing self-organization into their hierarchical, functionally organized company. It remains a secret as to how self-organization is supposed to develop under rigid prescribed structural conditions.

All of the findings from research on chaos and complexity suggest that excessive structuring and stable orders destroy the capacity of systems to organize themselves. Systems must be in a state of limited instability to be able to organize themselves. Only if systems are situated between (and beyond) stable balance and explosive chaos, the connections between their elements can arrange themselves in such a way that they contribute to the preservation of this overall structure. The chaos researcher Per Bak illustrates this process with the example of how sand piles form. If we let grains of sand fall on a specific point, the resulting system of a "sand pile" can develop three types of behavior that Bak calls sub-critical, critical, and over-critical. If the pile is still flat—the sub-critical state—then the falling grains of sand quickly come to rest; they may cause small, irregular avalanches. As the pile grows, it reaches a critical state. The falling grains of sand begin to organize themselves. Grains trigger avalanches that distribute the sand in regular patterns. Depending on the system's "need," the size of these avalanches can vary between one grain and the entire pile surface. This flexible, self-organizing behavior enables the pile to retain the same form, even during further growth. The slope of the pile is constant, independent of its size. If we put barriers on the side to influence the growth of the pile, the slope flattens. The pile system reaches an over-critical state in which self-organization can only develop in a restricted way. The falling grains of sand no longer try to shape a specific form of a pile. If however we remove the artificial structuring, the pile system falls back into a critical state. The sudden removal of barriers releases a giant avalanche that causes the pile system to revert to its specific shape with a constant slope (cf. Ruthen 1993: 135). It becomes clear that the increase in complexity moves the system from a sub-critical, orderly state into a critical state in which it can develop its capacity for self-organization. Structural impositions from outside can lead to an over-critical status in which the capacity for self-organization is lost again.

The beginning of the fall semester at many universities clearly illustrates how important the attainment of a critical state is for a system's ability to self-organize. Masses of new students stream into the lecture halls and seminar rooms, student housing shortages become acute, and the universities are bursting at the seams. Student representatives try again and again to draw attention to these circumstances with protests. Yet typically they can only get a tired smile from their fellow students, who are engaged in the daily struggle for grades, seats in courses, and housing. When critical mass is reached, there is suddenly major dynamism: students who were previously completely inactive occupy entire universities, organize seminars and lectures themselves, and take over university operations in the form of self-administration. Sudden mass protests in universities typically cannot be explained by a particularly awful situation. Even new, radical university development plans, particularly arrogant ministers of education, or positive experiences with protest in other countries suffice on their own to draw a student out. Frequently, the situation is not much better nor much worse in the years before and after a major wave of protests at universities. How can we explain the sudden emergence of student movements? There are events, the details of which are unimportant, that nonetheless have a self-amplifying dynamic, and they push the student body into a critical state in which its ability to self-organize comes into full bloom. In the moment in which students take up the scepter in a few departments, this can unleash a wave of action through the university landscape. Previously buried self-management abilities are used to organize connections between the individual students, departments, and universities. Networks of the most varied groups and individuals arise, people who probably did not know they had anything to do with one another.[20]

Managers have experiences, often unanticipated ones, with the capability for self-organization in systems in critical status. Endenburg Elektrotechniek, for example, reached a critical state during the shipyards crisis of the 1970s in which the ability of workers to self-organize could manifest itself. At the highpoint of the shipyards crisis of 1976, the Rotterdam-based company's order book was empty. Midsized shipyards, the most important customer group at this time, had to surrender to the pressure of low-cost competition from the Far East, or tried to keep their heads above water with repair work. Sixty employees in the Fabricage department who specialized in shipbuilding faced losing their jobs. Instead of moving forward with the implementation of the redundancy plan, which had already been drafted, the company's leadership and employees decided to find new applications for their products and to expand their services portfolio. The employees went out on their own to get orders from construction sites and to create new fields of activity for the expertise they had gained in shipbuilding. During this time, Endenburg Elektrotechniek developed the first radar-supported security systems and expanded into the market for emergency power systems.

The process of self-organization no longer refers primarily to elements that comprise a system, but rather on the interrelationships that can development in systems. In the process of self-organization, the parts or elements are no longer important; instead, what matters is the actions and interactions that issue from them. An organization is no longer the sum of its parts; it is a complex structure of actions and interactions between independent elements. The U.S. organizational consultant Russell L. Ackoff (1994) long ago proposed the following mental game to illustrate this idea: We buy 555 different automobiles, hire the best available engineers, and tell them to identify the best engine, the best transmission, the best chassis, the best vehicle body, etc., from among the 555 models. Once the engineers have found the best parts, we tell them to use them to build the "best possible automobile." We'll find out that this hybrid cobbled together of Rolls-Royce, Jaguar, Honda, BMW, Mercedes and Fiat can't even hold up to an Opel Mantra. The parts just don't fit together into a powerful whole. The performance of a system is not the sum of the performances of its individual parts; it is the product of the interaction between the parts. This shift in central perspectives from the performances of individual parts to the ways in which these parts interact with one another raises the question for managers and consultants as to how we can design these interrelations in such a way that they serve the preservation and further development of the entire system.

5.2 The Search Strategies of Post-bureaucratic Organizations

Self-organization, orientation towards face-to-face interactions, feedback loops, irregular patterns, the impossibility of long-term predictions, organizations in limited instability—these are all explanatory approaches that are meant to contribute to an improved understanding of post-bureaucratic organizations. It is precisely because it is no longer quite so simple to identify and manage processes in organizations beyond hierarchy and anarchy that the need for new points of reference continues to grow. Recourse to findings from research on chaos and complexity should stimulate considerations about how a new kind of thinking in management would look: to develop visions and versions of the future without falling into the trap of long-term planning; to focus not on attaining objectives, but rather the exploitation of spontaneously arising possibilities; to prepare for various opportunities without having to rely on the occurrence of specific developments;

thinking in feedback loops, analogies, and irregular patterns, not in causal connections and quantifiable contexts; concentration not on the performance of individual elements of an organization, but rather on the ways in which they interact.

The dissemination of a new vocabulary derived from research on chaos and complexity among managers, employees, and organizational consultants seems to suggest that this issue is not in the past. Organizational management teams are looking for opportunities to shape themselves in such a way that this kind of thinking can unfold—and that space is freed up that can be used for processes of self-organization. Post-bureaucratic organizations face the challenge of creating these free spaces without falling victim to the dilemmas of identity, politicization, and complexity. It would be illusory to believe that there are forms of organization that would enable us to completely avoid the dilemmas inherent in post-bureaucratic organizations. There are no magic formulas for free spaces without risks. In recent decades, however, experiments by post-bureaucratic organizations have shown that there seem to be structures that are more apt than others.

There have been various attempts to organize (reduce) uncertainty without the organization having to give up its capacity for self-organization. The displacement of uncertainty can occur both in the form of externalization to the exterior world and in the form of internalization into the interior world. The externally directed strategy aims to outsource certain organizational fields (that are burdened with uncertainty); the goal of internalization is to relegate uncertainty (and dealing with it) to employees, thereby relieving the organization.

In the process, new forms of formalized structures emerge that attempt to come to grips with the paradox of simultaneous stability and flexibility. The following discussion focuses on three strategies with which organizations have experimented in recent decades to reduce uncertainty without destroying their capacity for self-organization from the beginning: outsourcing, technologization, and context management. None of these are panaceas for post-bureaucratic organizations, and these concepts—as research shows—come with several stumbling blocks. Despite their problems, however, they point to ways in which post-bureaucratic organizations can at least get a partial hold on the dilemmas of identity, politicization, and complexity.

Outsourcing

The establishment of profit and service centers merely represents a displacement of uncertainties toward the interior, but the coordination and communication problems of such centers affect the overall organization all the same in a secondary way. In the coordination mechanisms between the organization's center and decentralized centers, we find structures that deliver a high degree of flexibility, yet on the other hand guarantee a minimum degree of stability. The economization of relations between the center and profit or service centers is based on a simulation of markets. Every communication between the core and the centers should be translated into economic semantics if possible. Every transaction, whether it involves products, people, or tasks, is translated into monetary values.

The strategy of externalizing uncertainty while simultaneously upholding a minimum degree of control over outsourced organizational parts can only work if the organization manages to situate the profit center in the border region between the organization and the exterior world. Outsourced profit centers have to be two things at once: a contractual relationship between autonomous stakeholders (for example, two companies cooperating on research), and a stand-alone formal organization. This means that an outsourced profit center's activity is subject to a dual orientation at the most basic level: it has to generate profit as a stand-alone unit while also increasing the prosperity of the group. An action is therefore attributed both to the autonomous unit and to the entire organization.

The relationship between the autonomy of the profit center and loyalty to the group is not stable. Profit centers tend to develop into independent collective stakeholders. By developing self-referential relationships, meaning referring all internal organizational processes inwards to itself, independent organizational units have the opportunity to move away from the companies that control them. This potential arises because there are real synergistic phenomena underway in networks of organized profit centers: the whole is more than the sum of its parts. The characteristics of networks consisting of profit centers can no longer be explained by the participating elements; instead, they must be understood as the result of a self-organizing process dynamic. The market networks consisting of profit centers are located not just "in between," but rather "beyond" contract and organization (Teubner 1992: 190). It is this synergy or emergence effect that enables post-bureaucratic organizations to successfully navigate an extremely turbulent environment. The "knotting together" of organizational processes with external uncertainties (and opportunities) leads to a situation in which these external uncertainties can be brought under control.

This development finds its most extreme expression in "clover-leaf organizations" and "virtual organizations." The clover leaf organization—a term coined by the consultant Charles Handy (1990)—consists of a core organization in which only a few highly-paid coordinators work, while the lion's share of the work is done by subcontractors who are paid on the basis of their results rather than for their time. At peak times, flexible manpower is added for a brief time. Virtual companies consist primarily of a complex information system and sub-companies. The business journalist John A. Byrne (1993) and the consultant William H. Davidow (with Malone 1992) identify technology, peak performance, trust, and the short term as important features of virtual companies. Companies that can deliver outstanding performance by concentrating on their core competences connect to one another by using new information and communication technologies. Because a service is provided jointly, the relationships must be trusting (see Grey/Garsten 2001). However, the relationships exist only as long as the joint service is being provided. Once the order is fulfilled, the relationship is dissolved. In the final analysis, these organizational principles amount to "hollow organizations," the single purpose of which is to serve as a gearshift between various stakeholders. This gives rise to organizations that buy their ideas rather than develop them themselves, that hand off production to subcontractors, and that organize distribution through independent sales agents.[21]

One example of this kind of company is a shipping firm that does not have its own trucks and drivers; instead, they only work with a complex electronic logistics system and subcontractors. Another example are intermediary companies that buy "their" product ideas from design companies and hand over production and packaging to a supplier in Hong Kong that then outsources work-intensive production processes to small businesses. Independent sales representatives conduct sales, and even the company's financial liabilities are sold to specialized debt collectors.

The great risk of organizing value creation processes along the lines of the market, however, is that the coordinating companies, which frequently hold power by virtue of this coordinating role, cannot resist the urge to intervene in units that are actually independent. Too many parent companies that subscribe to profit center logic still cherish the dream—fully within the Taylorist tradition—of establishing absolute certainty regarding the behavior of independent units. They want to have the final word despite relationships with autonomous entities that are rooted in market terms and are therefore precariously organized. They therefore attempt to reorganize the company divisions that were just outsourced, which are actually now subject to market conditions, and from the perspective of a company in such a way that the uncertainties remain solely with the profit centers and sub-companies. Large final manufacturers, for example in the metalworking industry, often have such a strong position of power vis-à-vis their suppliers that they can impose demands on these officially independent companies as to how they shape their internal processes for operational division of labor, staff allocation, and training.

An especially good example of this strategy is the relationship between oil companies and "their" officially independent gas stations: the people who lease the gas stations, who the oil companies grandly refer to as station managers, are provided with property and a building shell free of charge. Yet these can be taken away at any time. The leaseholder has to set up the gas station on their own and buy a basic inventory of products, for which they take out a loan. The oil company does not just force the leaseholder to accept a prescribed volume of their own gasoline; they also require the leaseholder to buy products for their gas station shop from

the oil company at inflated prices. These contractually stipulated relationships enable nearly complete control over the leaseholders. As soon as
they earn more money than the company is willing to allow, the leasing
fee increases. Oil companies scrupulously ensure that leaseholder profits
cannot guarantee a life (that would lower corporate profits), nor lead to
death (that would only be somewhat sensible). Because of the debt that
leaseholders assume when they enter into the relationship, however, there
is scarcely an option to get out of this unequal contract. Excessive leasing
fees that are adjusted to profits indirectly squeeze out the maximum from
gas station leaseholders. This forces leaseholders to hire illicit workers and
to violate laws governing operating hours for businesses, whether this is
on the margins or simply outside of legal bounds. When these few cases
come to light, oil companies are then able to wash their hands of it and
dismiss the leaseholder as a black sheep, now deep in debt, from the lease
agreement. The company headquarters use this assignment of work to
subcontractors and profit centers not just to derive efficiency advantages,
but also to effect illegitimate risk displacement and liability limitations
(Teubner 1992: 209). The system of "independent" gas station tenants
shows the ways in which a company can reduce internal uncertainties
(and increase profits).

   In virtual companies, the shifting of uncertainties to formally independent profit centers is taken to an extreme: The independent sub-
contractor in a virtual shipping company is the only one who sticks his
neck out for constant speeding to meet deadlines, which seem more
real than virtual to the driver. Although the "vampire technique" of
oil companies or virtual transportation companies promises short-term
profits, long-term success remains extremely dubious. It is not just that
discontented gas station leaseholders and truck drivers who feel they
have been treated unjustly can endanger the prosperity of a more or
less virtual company over the long term; it is also that the opportunities
inherent to company relationships organized along market lines are not
fully exploited by this underlying winner-loser logic. The creativity of
independent units and their capacity for self-organization are unnec-
essarily pared down, and important own initiatives are inhibited or
directed at how best one can trick the virtual parent company.

Post-bureaucratic Architecture: A Means of Mechanization

We have already assessed the ambivalence of mechanization: the possibility of generating stability on one hand and flexibility on the other. Technologization and mechanization were central instruments of control for work processes in bureaucratic organizations: The will to dominate was "deeply impressed upon machines and organizations" (Gorz 1973: 12). In this form of organization, mechanization was understood as a process with which subtle, imperceptible, and therefore all the more effective forms of exercising power could be established. Mechanization contributes to creating stability. As Luhmann writes, it leads to relief for meaning-processing processes of experience and action from the acceptance, formulation, and communicative explication of all connotations that are implied (Luhmann 1979). The introduction of the typewriter, in a simple example from the organizational theorist Charles Perrow (1986), rendered the previously existing rules about the size and shape of letters superfluous. The introduction of graphics computers made it unnecessary for engineering students to go to great pains to learn precisely standardized lettering for labeling machines designed on the drawing board. Computer programs now take care of the precisely defined rounding and spacing for letters that was previously governed by norms. Information and communications technology has further revolutionized this principle. It can be used to pre-program formal rules, bureaucratic procedures, and external controls. Procedures that previously required laborious negotiations and were set down in writing can now be integrated into computer software, technical languages, and codes.

This simplification of processes through mechanization, however, creates a new complexity at a higher level. On one hand, an organization can harness new opportunities created by this "relief"; however, it must also confront new coordination needs outside of the processes directly affected by mechanization: the technology must be produced and installed, inspected and maintained. The irony of mechanization and automation is that although technology can simplify elementary processes and avoid first-order mistakes, yet it also requires controls at a higher level and monitoring of second-order mistakes (Bainbridge 1987).

Exposed to demands for flexibility and innovation, organizations seem to see the necessity of designing the mechanization process in as open a way as possible. The creation of stability through mechanization and the later usage of this technology must be closely aligned: computer programs, for example, have to give the user the option to program repetitions themselves (and even if only through the creation of printing format templates in text processing). Rough structures are framed in which the maximum degree of flexibility is enabled. The best computer program would accordingly be a program that allows users to do everything within their remit (for example, data administration). The design of buildings for post-bureaucratic organizations impressively illustrates how mechanization can do justice to demands for both stability and flexibility.

The architecture of Taylorist-Fordist organizations was oriented towards total control. The aesthetic of their buildings was meant to express the attitude and spirit that was intended: the emphasis on hierarchy. Rooms were designed in such a way that people could see them from a central position and could have immediate access to workers. There arose an "architecture of discipline" (Foucault 1977) that basically did not differ from prisons and psychiatric institutions. In post-bureaucratic organizations, this kind of architecture would be devastating, according to management. Management also claims that an organization oriented towards flexibility cannot develop in the same rooms in which years' worth of separation and control sought to establish eternal stability. Eberhard Schnelle suggests the potential inherent in architecture to support processes of transformation: "Architecture can make an essential contribution to stimulate communication among managers and administrators. The philosophy of incorporating participants in an open phase of the decision-making process should find expression in architecture." Schnelle strives toward an architecture that facilitates group work of all kinds, all sizes, and for every purpose. The proposed heart of this "new communication architecture" is a forum as a central, open location for all kinds of events—for spontaneous exchanges of ideas, small congresses, information markets, symposia, presentations, and much more (early on, Schnelle 1989: 8; a critical response in Saval 2014: 200ff.).

Context Management

In management literature, context management means "the reflexive decentralized control of context conditions in all partial systems and autonomous self-control for every individual partial system" (Wilke 1989b: 86). The discrete units are involved as decentralized stakeholders in the formulation of a superimposed pattern. This participation in the determination of superimposed patterns—for example in commissions, ad hoc groups, integrative authorities—creates the prerequisite for orienting respective self-control towards the premises of context management. It constitutes a "commitment device by means of participation" (Wilke 1989b: 86f.). This provides the basis for the idea in management that the coordination of collective activity is possible if the organization's members communicate with one another on a voluntary basis. The exchange of expectations, needs, information, and interests is meant to facilitate the joint definition and attainment of objectives (Wilke 1989a: 135ff.). Management believes that this form of management could do away with the dilemma of differentiation caused by the division of labor and replace it with a "combination of participation and self-commitment."

The principle of context management has been implemented in organizations through the principles of sociocracy and holacracy. Working groups and control groups are decision-making bodies that determine the entire company policy. As Gerard Endenburg emphasizes, these groups should not just make it easier to "achieve consensus before the decision," but also "the later implementation of resolutions made within the 'normal' hierarchical structure." The working groups consist of two representatives from each individual department. One of them is the head of department named by the working group, and the other is one of the delegates selected by the department staff. This was supposed to simplify the "gearing of different levels of superstructure"; at least this was the hope of the sociocratic Endenburg (1992: 139).

The "dogma" of the consensus principle, the double bond, and the selection of the staff is meant to provide an organizational answer to a fundamental problem of context management. In context management, we assume that the process of coordinating between vertically differentiated units may be rife with conflict, yet is possible in a relatively problem-free way. The coordination between different units would only become unproblematic if the rationalities were the same across all of the units. We know from the work of Richard M. Cyert and James G. March (1963), however, that there are only local rationalizations in organizations that we find in organizations as a mere collection of partial rationalities, if we find anything at all. If there is not something like a superimposed rationality, then the process of negotiating patterns can only ever be finding compromise. This calls for mechanisms that make it possible for all participants to agree with the result of the pattern or context formation. Otherwise, the principle of context management would fail. In the sociocratic or holocratic model, we are talking in the final analysis about a dogmatic determination of a process for the building of organizational patterns. The secured formalization of this process first creates the framework for the ability to do justice to the fact that partially autonomous units also really accept the pattern or context.

5.3 We Are Only at the Beginning—Looking Forward

Whenever managers, consultants, or scholars argue that hierarchical management in organizations are being replaced with increasing frequency by other forms of control, they are working with very strict differentiations: Organizations choose between decentralization *or* centralization, solo work *or* group work, hierarchicalization *or* de-hierarchicalization, hierarchical control *or* market controls.

There are, however, tendencies to that effect to increasingly dissolve strict analytical differentiations. Paradoxical-sounding formulations such as "controlled autonomy," "centralized decentralization," "bureau-cratic de-bureaucratization," "forced freedom," "managed autonomy," "managed self-management," or "externally organized self-organi-zation" proclaim the compatibility of decentralized and centralized management, and of hierarchical and non-hierarchical mechanisms of control.

These paradoxes allude to the fact that control via hierarchy is the central medium for the coordination of non-hierarchical forms of coordination such as the market or common understanding. Within an organization, hierarchy can be used very effectively to demon-strate authority that is not bound to the conditions of inferiority or superiority. Niklas Luhmann (1964: 161ff.) has suggested that this kind of non-hierarchical, derived authority is a central mechanism for managing decision-making processes. This means for example that a manager whose authority is grounded in hierarchy can arrange things in such a way that a project group in an administration should make decisions solely through internal, consensual understanding. Or that a manager has the option of issuing a directive within a company that cooperative relationships between units should be conducted through market mechanisms.

From this perspective, it is understandable during organizational reforms that the decentralization of responsibility is frequently accom-panied by a centralization of competences at the top of the organiza-tion. The decentralization of decision-making competence, in terms of the form that work and order processing take, leads to a loss of control at the top of the organization, to which they react with centralization strategies. This splitting into a variety of different autonomous units tends to lead toward the intensified formation of local rationalities, which the organization's leadership tries to confront with central inte-gration strategies, such as organizational mission statements. The dis-mantling of hierarchical mechanisms of control, such as introducing group work, project teams, or profit centers, leads to new processes of coordination that are managed in a hierarchical way. The groups, project teams, and profit centers have to coordinate among them-selves. To do this, new hierarchical instruments of control are typically created. The definition of framework conditions for internal markets, the determination of rules for cooperation between work groups, and the introduction of targets may not be classical, hierarchical modes of making assignments, but this is clearly about the hierarchical control of an organization.

In organizations, there are manifold examples for these kinds of centralized decentralization and hierarchical management of non-hierarchical coordination mechanisms. Process optimizations in the field of production with the Kaizen method may be arranged by the central office, but the process optimizations themselves are no longer in the hands of external rationalization experts; they are implemented instead by employees themselves in a decentralized manner. The introduction of group work leads to a decentralization of decision-making competences and a reduction of middle management. At the same time, however, certain instruments for creating financial figures are centralized to facilitate better hierarchical control of the groups. The creation of profit centers intends to lead to the formation of local organizational cultures. However, the upper echelons of the organization invest a great deal of money at the same in a frequently futile effort to establish a uniform organizational culture.[22]

From the perspective on the entire organization, we can hardly speak of a "crisis of hierarchy," a "hierarchical dead-end," or even an "end of hierarchy." "Dehierarchalization," when focused on an entire organization, clearly leads to disorientation (see Rhodes/Price 2011). Despite all of the anti-hierarchy rhetoric in many organizations and in the writings of management gurus, no organization with more than fifty or sixty employees has fully done away with hierarchy. When push comes to shove, every organization has the option of implementing a decision centrally. Whenever it comes to putting sensitive decisions into action, people always reach for hierarchy, even if it has become taboo.

When dealing with organizations, we are far more often facing a modification of hierarchical instruments of management. The central conflict about organizational forms revolves around which mechanisms of coordination and control should be used to process single work steps in the context of an uncontested overall hierarchical regulation.

It is only at this point—in individual work processes—that hierarchy comes under pressure to legitimate itself as a management mechanism.

Organizations have to justify even more vehemently the fact that control and coordination expense for individual work processes are best solved by means of hierarchy, and not through other forms of management such as market controls or understandings. These forms of hierarchy can be described as "fluctuating hierarchy" or "functional hierarchy." "Fluctuating hierarchical control" is understood as a constellation in which management and coordination is not performed predominantly at the top of the organization. Instead, management and coordination competences are "bundled" at the levels of hierarchy where the problems lie. It largely depends on the type of problem as to whether management and coordination are done by means of hierarchical, market-based, or discursive regulations. "Functional hierarchical control" is understood as a strategy of only providing these services through hierarchy, if hierarchy was able to legitimate itself previously as a suitable form of coordination. Hierarchy is not allowed to enjoy unquestioned dominance as a form of control in specific work processes; instead, hierarchy must prevail as an appropriate form in contrast to functional equivalents for managing an organization. Or: hierarchical mechanisms of control are no longer viewed as set; instead, hierarchy must be able to prove its superiority as the more suitable form of controlling discrete work processes.

This seems to cause a change in the forms of power conflicts in organizations. In a fully hierarchical Taylorist organization, attention was focused on the question of who assumed what position in the hierarchy and what level of managerial authority is assigned to each hierarchical position. If the staffing of the hierarchical position and its authority to issue directives was unanimously agreed, there is a clear framework for decision-making processes. This seems to change by means of processes of decentralization and dehierarchization. In the framework of a generally accepted hierarchical overall control, conflicts no longer occur regarding the question of who occupies which hierarchical position and with what powers the position is endowed; increasingly often, conflicts are related to the question of which control media will be used to tackle specific work processes. Discussions about group work, profit centers, manufacturing segments, internal customer relationships, project teams, and quality circles are then always power struggles about whether internal processes should be regulated with the control media of professional influence, understanding, internal markets, trust, and/or hierarchy.

In all of the drama staged by managers and consultants, changes in organizations move within the range of a basic hierarchical order that is accepted by almost all stakeholders. The discussion about new forms of organization should not distract us from the fact that there is no indication at all that there has been a drop in hierarchical order within organizations. The "revolution from above," the "auto-disempowerment of hierarchies," is not happening in organizations.

Afterword on methodology

In this book, I chose to use the display side of organizations as the point of departure for my remarks. I attempt to show what the effects would be if the principles presented on the display side were implemented on a one-to-one basis. Even if we use organizational theory to carry the principles promulgated on this display side to their logical conclusions, it becomes clear that an organization would then confront fundamentally new problems if they were to implement these principles.

These structural problems—summed up under the keywords of the identity, politicization, and complexity dilemma—can explain why the principles propagated on the display side only find expression in a weakened form in the formal structure. By showing the form in which management concepts, celebrated with glossy pictures, are actually implemented in the formal structure, I hope to have given a realistic look at what really changes in an organization.

Unwanted side effects of management concepts that are praised to the heavens on the display side are often balanced out by employees by means of informal procedures and actions that frequently contradict the formal rules. These informal mechanisms—hidden regulations or invisible hierarchies—have, in the rarest of cases, something to do with what is praised on the display side as a "very special organizational culture" among pioneering organizations.

I have relied on three sources for my books on organizational science: From my own research projects on organizations in which I pursued specific questions on new management concepts; from consulting projects that, as a sort of waste product, provided interesting insights into organizations; and from descriptive reports that were prepared by other consultants, managers, or scholars about a specific organization.

In this book, I relied heavily on the last body of sources: descriptions of organizations by other consultants, managers, and scholars. Because it is a typical practice in the management literature not to

anonymize the organizations under analysis, I identify those organizations with their real names. If the examples in the published literature
were anonymized, then I follow the authors of these studies and use
their pseudonyms, even if I know the real name of the organization.
A few of the examples introduced in the book are based on my own
empirical research that I have collected as a researcher, consultant, and
in some cases even as a member of an organization. In these cases, I
have either elided the names of the organizations or invented fictional
names for them.

Notes

1 Unlike the distinction between two sides that predominates in organizational theory, I believe it is necessary to distinguish between three sides when systematically analyzing organizations (Kühl 2013: 87ff.).

2 Anna Pollert (1988: 218ff.) has already pointed out this problem in her discussion of "flexible firms."

3 For a collection of such early reports on pioneering companies, see the volume of Daft 1992. It was particularly ironic that, because of the long production time for books, the McKinsey consultants Richard Foster and Sarah Kaplan (2001) praised the Enron book as a successful model for all other companies, just as the accounting tricks of their former McKinsey colleagues and former Enron CEO Jeff Skilling came to light and the firm was already bankrupt. For more on such cases of dual realities in capital-market-oriented companies, see Kühl 2005.

4 We can illustrate this assumption with a simple idea from cybernetics. W. Ross Ashby (1956), one of the fathers of cybernetics who organizational practitioners often like to cite, discovered that organizations are forced to bring their own inner structure into harmony with external requirements. The complex environment—which in the final analysis means nothing more than a contradictory environment—constantly "tests" the organization's ability to change, and organizations that are not in a position to handle this contradictory nature are "punished" with failure. This is merely a brief summary of Ashby from the literature. For early connections to Ashby, see for example Cameron 1980.

5 On the ways in which management gurus function, see Clark/ Bhatanacharoen/Greatbatch 2012.

6 This was already clear in the 1990s after the failure of the first re-engineering and Lean Management projects. See as an example

the CSC Index 1994; Scott-Morgan 1994. There are significantly more interesting analyses in the anthology of Knights/Willmott 2000.

7 I am referring here to explanations for the failure of re-engineering and Lean Management projects in the 1990s; see Harvey 1994; Champy 1995.

8 Here I am referring to discussions in the labor process debate, in which it is assumed that managers have a tendency towards independence from the will of workers, meaning that managers consequently lean towards direct control and automation (see the prominent participations in this discussion: Edwards 1979; Friedman 1977, and Burawoy 1979).

9 I am dealing here jointly with the approaches of Scientific Management and bureaucratic theory, despite a few differences. Both sides are the result of a belief in the "omnipotence" of redundancy-producing processes, both in terms of their origin and their basic assumptions.

10 These ideas can be connected with the entire discussion about the control of workers. In the confrontation with bureaucratic, hierarchical, Taylorist and Fordist forms of businesses, both proponents and opponents discussed coordination and regulation in the same breath as control (cf. for example Edwards 1979: 12ff.).

11 On the character of resolute decision-making premises as formal expectations in organizations, see Kühl 2013: 94ff.

12 It is also possible to imagine the reverse case. A complex technology is a potential factor of uncertainty, and a human worker guarantees that this technology functions properly. Exceptions (Chernobyl, Seveso, Bhopal, Hoechst) tragically confirm this rule.

13 There was a veritable boom of publications on semi-autonomous work groups at the end of the 1980s and the early 1990s; see for example Manz/Sims 1987: 107; Manz/Keating/Donnellon 1990: 15; Millot/Roulleau 1991: 13; Schilder 1992: 67.

14 This is why Mats Alvesson and Hugh Willmott (1996) describe Business Process Reengineering as a "totalizing solution." On Lean Management, see Holweg's informative 2007 work.

15 This point is of course exaggerated. Naturally, the resistance put up by middle management and the adjustment difficulties among employees play a role that cannot be ignored in the introduction of new organizational forms. The focus on these points however obscures insight into the deeper problem that post-bureaucratic organizations move "at the limit of their existential possibilities" due to their loose internal linkages.

16 Luhmann would probably reject the description of decisions as "within the meaning of the organization" as too imprecise. Luhmann believes that all of the actions of mental and social systems are subjected to a "diktat of the meaningful." If were to describe actions as "within the meaning" of an organization, I want to point out that every specific meaning "qualifies itself by suggesting specific possibilities of connection and making others improbable, difficult, remote, or (temporarily) excluded (Luhmann 1984: 94f.—English translation Luhmann 1995, p. 79). "Meaningful" or "not meaningful" therefore refer to the fact that meaning only gains reality when it is referenced to another meaning.

17 Meaning is a central category of Luhmann's systems theory. Without meaning, mental systems, organizations, even all of society, would simply cease to exist (Luhmann 1971: 11). These systems would fail because they are no longer in a position to delimit themselves from the overwhelming complexity of the exterior environment.

18 Exceptions prove the rule here. The infamous Church of Scientology has managed not only to preserve its solvency by means of religious fulfillment, ideological propriety, moral uprightness, and ultimate truthfulness, but also to make profits (at the cost of its members and "client" companies) that other firms can only dream of.

19 For an interesting case of how ideas about decentralization and flat hierarchies are implemented in armies, see Bjørnstad 2011.

20 On the concept of the tipping point, see the highly readable overview by Malcolm Gladwell (2000). The transfer of this concept to organizational research has not yet advanced very far.

21 Knoke 2001 offers a good overview of different network organizations at 120ff.

22 Accordingly, it is not surprising that both bureaucratic and post-bureaucratic structural features occur in the same organization; see for example Hodgson 2004; Bolin/Härenstam 2008, or Farrell/Morris 2013.

Bibliography

Ackoff, Russell L. (1994), The Humane Corporation: Integrating Work, Play, and Learning, New York/Oxford: Oxford University Press.

Alvesson, Mats/Thompson, Paul (2005), Postbureaucracy?, in: Stephen Ackroyd/Rosemary Batt/Paul Thompson/Pamela S. Tolbert (eds.), The Oxford Handbook of Work and Organization, Oxford: Oxford University Press, 485–507.

Alvesson, Mats/Willmott, Hugh (1996), Making Sense of Management: A Critical Introduction, London/Thousand Oaks/New Delhi: Sage.

Aoki, Masahiko (1988), Information, Incentives and Bargaining in the Japanese Economy, Cambridge: Cambridge University Press.

Ashby, W. Ross (1956), An Introduction to Cybernetics, New York: John Wiley.

Atlan, Henri (1979), Entre le Cristal et la Fumée, Paris: Seuil.

Baecker, Dirk (1992), Fehldiagnose „Überkomplexität". Komplexität ist die Lösung, nicht das Problem, in: GDI Impuls 4, 55–62.

Bainbridge, Lisanne (1987), Ironies of Automation, in: Jens Rasmussen/Keith Duncan/Jacques Leplat, (eds.), New Technology and Human Error, Chicester: Wiley, 271–283.

Barker, James R. (1993), Tightening the Iron Cage: Concertive Control in Self-Managing Teams, in: Administrative Science Quarterly 38, 408–437.

Barker, James R. (1999), The Discipline of Teamwork. Participation and Concertive Control, London/Thousand Oaks/ New Delhi: Sage.

Bell, Daniel (1973), The Coming Post-Industrial Society. A Venture in Social Forecasting, New York: Basic Book.

Bennis, Warren G. (1966), The Coming Death of Bureaucracy, in: Think Magazine 11–12, 30–35.

Berrebi-Hoffmann, Isabelle (1990), Le management culturel de face et de profil, in: Annales de mines 21, 4–12.

Berger, Ulrike (1988), Rationalität, Macht und Mythen, in: Willi Küpper/Günther Ortmann (eds.), Mikropolitik. Rationalität, Macht und Spiele in Organisationen, Opladen: WDV, 115–130.

Bjørnstad, Anne L. (2011), Exploring Network Organization in Military Contexts. Effects of Flatter Structure and More Decentralized Processes, in: Military Psychology 23, 315–331.

Bolin, Malin/Härenstam, Annika (2008), An Empirical Study of Bureaucratic and Post-Bureaucratic Characteristics in 90 Workplaces, in: Economic and Industrial Democracy 29, 541–564.

Braverman, Harry (1974), Labor and Monopoly Capital: The Degradation of Work in the Twentieth Century, New York/London: Monthly Review Press.

Buck, John A./Endenburg, Gerard (1984), The Creative Forces of Self-Organization, Columbia, MD: Sociocratic Center.

Burnham, James (1941), The Managerial Revolution, New York: Day.

Burns, Tom/Stalker, Georg M. (1966), The Management of Innovation, 2. ed., London: Tavistock.

Buroway, Michael (1979), Manufacturing Consent, Chicago/London: University of Chicago Press.

Bush, John B./Frohman, Alan L. (1991), Communication in a "Network" Organization, in: Organizational Dynamics 3, 23–36.

Byrne, John A. (1993), The Virtual Corporation, in: International Businessweek 08.02.1993, 36–41.

Cameron, Kim S. (1980), Critical Questions in Assessing Organizational Effectiveness, in: Organizational Dynamics 9, 66–80.

Carlzon, Jan (1987), Moments of Truth: New Strategies for Today's Customer-Driven Economy, forward by Tom Peters, New York: HarperCollins and Cambridge, MA: Ballinger.

Champy, James (1995), Reengineering Management. The Mandate for New Leadership, New York: Harper Business.

Chandler, Alfred D. (1977), The Managerial Revolution in American Business, Cambridge, MA/London: Harvard University Press.

Chandler, Margaret K./Sayles, Leonard R. (1971), Managing Large Systems, New York: Harper & Row.

Child, Peter/Diederichs, Raimund/Sanders, Falk-Hayo/Wisniowski, Stefan (1991), SMR Forum: The Management of Complexity, in: Sloan Management Review 3, 73–80.

Clark, Timothy/Bhatanacharoen, Pojanath/Greatbatch, David (2012), Management Gurus as Celebrity Consultants, in: Matthias Kipping/ Timothy Clark (eds.), Management Consulting, Oxford/New York: Oxford University Press, 347–364.

Coriat, Benjamin (1991), Penser à l'envers, Paris: Christian Bourgois.

Crozier, Michel (1964), The Bureaucratic Phenomenon, Chicago: University of Chicago Press.

Crozier, Michel (1989), L'Entreprise à l'écoute: Apprendre le management postindustriel, Paris: Interéditions.

Crozier, Michel/Friedberg, Erhard (1977), L'acteur et le système. Les contraintes de l'action collective, Paris: Seuil.

CSC Index (1994), State of Reengineering Report, Cambridge: CSC.

Cyert, Richard M./March, James G. (1963), A Behavioral Theory of the Firm, Englewood Cliffs, NJ: Prentice Hall.

Daft, Richard L. (1992), Organization Theory and Design, 4. ed., Saint Paul: West Publishing Company.

David, Paul A. (1986), Understanding the Economics of QWERTY: The Necessity of History, in: William N. Parker (ed.), Economic History and Modern Economist, Oxford: Basil Blackwell, 30–49.

Davidow, William H./Malone, Michael S. (1992), The Virtual Corporation: Structuring and Revitalizing the Corporation for the 21st Century, New York: HarperCollins.

Dohse, Knuth/Jürgens, Ulrich/Malsch, Thomas (1985), Fertigungsnahe Selbstregulierung oder zentrale Kontrolle—Konzernstrategie im Restrukturierungsprozess der Automobilindustrie, in: Frieder Naschold (ed.), Arbeit und Politik—Gesellschaftliche Regulierung der Arbeit und der sozialen Sicherung, Frankfurt a.M./New York: Campus, 49–89.

Drucker, Peter F. (1990), The Emerging Theory of Manufacturing, in: Harvard Business Review 5 (May–June), 94–102.

Drucker, Peter F. (1992), The New Society of Organizations, in: Harvard Business Review 5, 95–104.

Eccles, Robert G./Nohria, Nitin (1992), Beyond the Hype: Rediscovering the Essence of Management, Cambridge, MA: Harvard Business School Press.

Edwards, Richard C. (1979), Contested Terrain, New York: Basic.

Endenburg, Gerard (1986), Dear Manager, Do You Have your Guiding Licence?, Rotterdam: Sociocratisch Centrum.

Endenburg, Gerard (1992), Soziokratie—Königsweg zwischen Diktatur und Demokratie, in: Jürgen Fuchs (ed.), Das biokybernetische Modell. Unternehmen als Organismen, Wiesbaden: Gabler, 135–149.

Farrell, Catherine/Morris, Jonathan (2013), Managing the Neo-Bureaucratic Organisation: Lessons from the UK's Prosaic Sector, in: The International Journal of Human Resource Management 24, 1376–1392.

Flynn, Randolph/McCombs, Tom/Elloy, David (1990), Staffing the Self-managing Work Team, in: Leadership and Organization Development Journal 11, 26–31.

Follett, Mary Parker (1941), Dynamic Administration: The Collected Papers of Mary Parker Follett, London: Sir Isaac Pitman and Sons.

Foster, Richard/Kaplan, Sarah (2001), Creative Destruction: Why Companies That Are Built to Last Underperform the Market—And How to Successfully Transform Them, New York: Doubleday/Random House.

Foucault, Michel (1977), Discipline & Punish: The Birth of the Prison, New York: Pantheon.

Friedberg, Erhard (1992), Les quatre dimensions de l'action organisée, in: Revue française de sociologie 33, 531–557.

Friedman, Andrew (1977), Industry and Labour, London: Macmillan.

Fuchs, Jürgen (1992), Das Unternehmen—lebender Organismus oder tote Institution?, in: Peter Fuchs (ed.), Das biokybernetische Modell: Unternehmen als Organismen, Wiesbaden: Gabler, 13–74.

Fuchs, Jürgen (1993), Nach dem Abbau jetzt der Umbau, in: Technische Rundschau 35, 24–29.

Galbraith, Jay R. (1973), Designing Complex Organizations, Reading, MA: Addison-Wesley.

Gebhardt, Eike (1991), Abschied von der Autorität. Die Manager der Postmoderne, Wiesbaden: Gabler Verlag.

Gee, James Paul/Hull, Glynda/Lankshear, Colin (1996), The New Work Order. Behind the Language of the New Capitalism, Boulder: Westview Press.

Giddens, Anthony (1982), Profiles and Critiques in Social Theory, London/Basingstoke: Macmillan.

Gladwell, Malcolm (2000), The Tipping Point. How Little Things Can Make a Big Difference, New York: Little, Brown.

Grey, Chris/Garsten, Christian (2001), Trust, Control and Post-Bureaucracy, in: Organization Studies 22/2, 229–250.

Gorz, André (1973), Critique de la Division du Travail, Paris: Seuil.

Hammer, Michael/Champy, James (1993), Reengineering the Corporation: A Manifesto for Business Revolution, New York: HarperCollins.

Handy, Charles (1990), The Age of Unreason, Boston: Harvard Business School Press.

Harvey, David (1994), Reengineering: The Critical Success Factors, London: Wimbledon.

Heckscher, Charles (1994), Defining the Post Bureaucratic Type, in: Charles Heckscher/Anne Donnellon (eds.), The Post Bureacratic Organization: New Perspectives on Organizational Change, Thousand Oaks: Sage, 14–62.

Heydebrand, Wolf (1989), New Organizational Forms, in: Work and Occupation 16, 323–357.

Hirschhorn, Larry/Gilmore, Thomas (1992), The New Boundaries of the 'Boundaryless' Company, in: Harvard Business Review (May–June), 4–16.

Hodgson, Damian E. (2004), Project Work: The Legacy of Bureaucratic Control in the Post-Bureaucratic Organization, in. Organization 11, 81–100.

Holbeche, Linda (2015), The Agile Organization: How to Build an Innovative, Sustainable and Resilient Business, London: Kogan Page.

Holweg, Matthias (2007), The Genealogy of Lean Production, in: Journal of Operations Management 25, 420–437.

Horton, Robert B. (1990), Planning for Surprise. BP's Project 1990 is Built on Simplicity, Teamwork, and Trust, in: Industry Week 06.08.1990, 27.

Jarillo, J. Carlos (1988), On Strategic Networks, in: Strategic Management Journal 9, 31–41.

Johannisson, Bengt (1987), Anarchists and Organizers, Entrepreneurs in a Network Perspective, in: International Studies of Management & Organization 17, 90–127.

Johanson, Jan/Mattsson, Lars-Gunnar (1987), Interorganizational Relations in Industrial Systems: A Network Approach Compared with the Transaction-Cost Approach, in: International Studies of Management & Organization 17, 34–48.

Jung, Nicolas/Kieser, Alfred (2012), Consultants in the Management Fashion Arena, in: Matthias Kipping/Timothy Clark (eds.), Management Consulting, Oxford/New York: Oxford University Press, 327–346.

Kanter, Rosabeth Moss (1983), The Change Master: Innovation for Productivity in the American Corporation, New York: Simon & Schuster.

Knights, David/Willmott, Hugh (2000), The Reengineering Revolution? An Introduction, in: David Kinghts/Hugh Willmott (eds.), The Reengineering Revolution? Critical Studies of Corporate Change, London/Thousand Oaks/New Delhi: Sage, 1–25.

Knoke, David (2001), Changing Organizations: Business Networks in the New Political Economy, Boulder: Westview Press.

Kühl, Stefan (2005), Exit: How Venture Capital Changes the Laws of Economics, Working Paper 3/2005, http://www.uni-bielefeld.de/soz/personen/kuehl/pdf/Paper3.2005.-Exit-How-Venture-Capital-changes-the-Law-of-Economics.pdf

Kühl, Stefan (2013), Organizations: A Systems Approach, Farnham/Burlington, VT: Gower-Ashgate.

Laloux, Frederic (2014), Reinventing Organizations. A Guide to Creating Organizations Inspired by the Next Stage of Human Consciousness, Brussels: Nelson Parker.

Landier, Hubert (1989), L'entreprise polycellulaire. Pour penser l'entreprise de demain, Paris: Entreprise moderne d'édition.

Landier, Hubert (1991), Vers l'entreprise intelligente. Dynamique du changement et mutation du management, Paris: Calmann-Lévy.

Lawrence, Paul R./Lorsch, Jay W. (1967), Organization and Environment. Managing Differentiation and Integration, Homewood: Irwin.

Leue, Hennig (1989), Innovation und Zielorientierung. Analogien zwischen dem Geschehen in Jazzbands, Sinfonieorchestern und Unternehmern, Quickborn: Metaplan.

Lipietz, Alain (1993), Towards a New Economic Order: Postfordism, Ecology, and Democracy, Cambridge: Polity Press.

Likert, Rensis/Araki, Charles T. (1986), Managing Without a Boss: System 5, in: Leadership and Organization Development Journal 7, 17–20.

Linhart, Danièle (1991), Le torticolis de l'autruche. L'éternelle modernisation des entreprises françaises, Paris: Seuil.

Luhmann, Niklas (1964), Funktionen und Folgen formaler Organisation. Berlin: Duncker & Humblot.

Luhmann, Niklas (1969), Klassische Theorie der Macht. Kritik ihrer Prämissen, in: Zeitschrift für Politik 16, 393–402.

Luhmann, Niklas (1971), Moderne Systemtheorie als Form gesamtgesellschaftlicher Analyse, in: Jürgen Habermas/Niklas Luhmann (eds.), Theorie der Gesellschaft oder Sozialtechnologie—Was leistet die Systemforschung?, Frankfurt a.M.: Suhrkamp, 7–24.

Luhmann, Niklas (1975), Komplexität, in: Niklas Luhmann (ed.), Soziologische Aufklärung 2, Opladen: WDV, 204–220.

Luhmann, Niklas (1979), Trust and Power, Chichester: Wiley.

Luhmann, Niklas (1984), Soziale Systeme. Grundriss einer allgemeinen Theorie, Frankfurt a.M.: Suhrkamp.

Luhmann, Niklas (1995), Social Systems, Stanford: Stanford University Press.

Luhmann, Niklas (2000), Organisation und Entscheidung, Opladen: WDV.

Luhmann, Niklas (2003), Organization, in: Tore Bakken/Tor Hernes (eds.), Autopoietic Organization Theory: Drawing on Niklas Luhmann's Social Systems Perspective, Copenhagen et al.: Copenhagen Business School Press, 31–52.

Mandelbrot, Benoit B. (1983), The Fractal Geometry of Nature,

Manz, Charles C./Keating, David E./Donnellon, Anne (1990), Preparing for an Organizational Change to Employee Self-Management: The Managerial Transition, in: Organizational Dynamics 3, 15–26.

Manz, Charles C./Sims, Henry P. (1987), Leading Workers to Lead Themselves. The External Leadership of Self Managing Work Teams, in: Administrative Science Quarterly 32, 106–128.

Mayo, Elton (1948), The Human Problems of an Industrial Civilization, Boston: Division of Research Graduate School of Business Administration.

Meltzer, Hyman/Nord, Walter R. (eds.) (1981), Making Organizations Human and Productive. A Handbook for Practitioners, New York/Chichester/Brisbane/Toronto: John Wiley.

Millot, Michèle/Roulleau, Jean-Pol (1991), Transformer l'organisation du travail. L'autonomie créatrice, Paris: Les Éditions d'Organisation.

Mintzberg, Henry (1979), The Structuring of Organizations, Englewood Cliffs: Prentice-Hall.

Mintzberg, Henry (1988), The Adhocracy, in: James B. Quinn/Henry Mintzberg/Robert M. James (eds.), The Strategy Process. Concepts, Contexts, and Cases, Englewood Cliffs, NJ: Prentice Hall, 607–627.

Mintzberg, Henry/McHugh, Alexandra (1985), Strategy Formation in Adhocracy, in: Administrative Science Quarterly 30, 160–197.

Ouchi, William G. (1981), Theory Z. How American Business Can Meet the Japanese Challenge, New York: Addison-Wesley.

Palloix, Christian/Zarifian, Philippe (1989), La société postéconomique, Paris: L'Harmattan.

Perrow, Charles (1974), Is Business Really Changing?, in: Organizational Dynamics 2, 31–44.

Perrow, Charles (1986), Complex Organizations, 3. ed., New York: Random House.

Perrow, Charles (2007), Why Bureaucracy?, in: Amy S. Wharton (ed.), The Sociology of Organizations. An Anthology of Contemporary Theory and Research, Los Angeles: Roxbury Publishing Company, 23–51.

Peters, Thomas J. (1988a), Facing Up to the Need for a Management Revolution, in: California Management Review 2, 7–38.

Peters, Thomas J. (1988b), Thriving on Chaos: Handbook for a Management Revolution, New York: Harper & Row.

Peters, Thomas J. (1993), Jenseits der Hierarchien, in: Handelsblatt Junge Karriere 23.04.1993.

Piore, Michael J./Sabel, Charles F. (1984), The Second Industrial Divide: Possibilities for Prosperity, New York: Basic Books.

Pollert, Anna (1988), The "Flexible Firm". Fixation or Facts?, in: Work, Employment, and Society 2, 281–316.

Powell, Walter W. (2007), The Capitalist Firm in the Twenty-First Century. Emerging Patterns in Western Enterprise, in: Amy S. Wharton (ed.), The Sociology of Organizations. An Anthology of Contemporary Theory and Research, Los Angeles: Roxbury Publishing Company, 495–515.

Rammert, Werner (1988), Das Innovationsdilemma. Technikentwicklung im Unternehmen, Opladen: WDV.

Reeser, Clayton (1969), Some Potential Human Problems of Project Form of Organization, in: Academy of Management Journal 4, 459–467.

Rhodes, Carl/Price, O. Milani (2011), The Post-Bureaucratic Parasite: Contrasting Narratives of Organizational Change in Local Government, in: Management Learning 42, 241–260.

Robertson, Brian J. (2015), Holacracy. The New Management System for a Rapidly Changing World, New York: Holt.

Roever, Michael (1991), Tödliche Gefahr, in: Managermagazin 10, 218–232.

Rommel, Günter/Brück, Felix/Diederichs, Raimund (1993), Einfach überlegen. Das Unternehmenskonzept, das die Schlanken schlank und die Schnellen schnell macht, Stuttgart: Schäffer-Poeschel.

Rosenberg, Nathan (1963), Technological Change in the Machine Tool Industry, 1840–1910, in: Journal of Economic History 23/4 (December), 414–443; reprinted as chapter 1 in Nathan Rosenberg (1976), Perspectives on Technology, Cambridge: Cambridge University Press.

Ruthen, Russell (1993), Adapting to Complexity, in: Scientific American 1, 130–140.

Sainsaulieu, Renauld/Segrestin, Denis (1986), Vers une théorie sociologique de l'entreprise, in: Sociologie du travail 28, 335–350.

Saval, Nikil (2014), Cubed: A Secret History of the Workplace, New York: Doubleday.

Schilder, Jana (1992), Work Teams Boost Productivity, in: Personnel Journal 71/2, 67–71.

Schimank, Uwe (1986), Technik, Subjektivität und Kontrolle in formalen Organisationen. Eine Theorieperspektive, in: Rüdiger Seltz/Ulrich Mill (eds.), Organisationen als soziales System. Kontrolle und Kommunikationstechnologie in Arbeitsorganisationen, Berlin: Sigma, 71–92.

Schmidt, Jochen (1993), Die sanfte Organisations-Revolution. Von der Hierarchie zu selbststeuernden Systemen, Frankfurt a.M./New York: Campus.

Schnelle, Eberhard (1989), Architektur im Zeitalter der Kommunikation, Quickborn: Metaplan.

Schnelle, Wolfgang (1978), Interaktionelles Lernen—Wandel in der Fortbildung, Quickborn: Metaplan.

Scott, W. Richard (1981), Organizations: Rational, Natural, and Open Systems, Englewood Cliffs, NJ: Prentice Hall.

Scott-Morgan, Peter (1994), The Unwritten Rules of the Game: Master Them, Shatter Them, and Break Through the Barriers to Organizational Change, New York: McGraw-Hill.

Senge, Peter M. (1990), The Fifth Discipline: The Art and Practice of the Learning Organization, New York: Doubleday.

Simon, Herbert A. (1957), Models of Man. Social and Rational, New York: John Wiley & Sons.

Smith, Adam (1937), The Wealth of Nations, New York: Modern Library.

Stacey, Ralph D. (1992), Managing Chaos. Dynamic Business Strategies in an Unpredictable World, London: Kegan Paul.

Taylor, Frederick Winslow (1967), The Principles of Scientific Management, New York/London: Norton & Company.

Teubner, Gunther (1992), Die vielköpfige Hydra: Netzwerke als kollektive Akteure höherer Ordnung, in: Wolfgang Krohn/Günter Küppers (eds.), Emergenz. Die Entstehung der Ordnung, Organisation und Bedeutung, Frankfurt a.m.: Suhrkamp, 189–218.

Thompson, James D. (1967), Organizations in Action, New York: McGraw-Hill.

Thorelli, Hans B. (1986), Networks: Between Markets and Hierarchies, in: Strategic Management Journal 7, 37–51.

Tichy, Noel M. (1993), Handbook for Revolutionaries, appendix, in: Noel M. Tichy/Stratford Sherman (eds.), Control Your Destiny or Someone Else Will, New York: Doubleday, HarperCollins, 593–673.

Toffler, Alvin (1971), Future Shock, New York: Bantam Books.

Toffler, Alvin (1990), Powershift: Knowledge, Wealth, and Violence at the Edge of the 21st Century, New York: Bantam Books.

Tomaney, John (1994), A New Paradigm of Work Organization and Technology?, in: Ash Amin (ed.), Post-Fordism. A Reader, Oxford: Blackwell, 157–195.

Valery, Paul (1989), The Outlook for Intelligence, Princeton: Princeton University Press.

Vaziri, M. T. (1987), Productivity Improvement through Quality Control Circles: A Comparative Approach, in: Leadership and Organizational Development Journal 8, 17–19.

Waalkes, Otto (1984), Das Buch Otto, München: Heyne.

Waldrop, M. Mitchell (1992), Complexity: Life at the Edge of Chaos, New York: Simon & Schuster.

Warnecke, Hans-Jürgen (1993), The Fractal Company: A Revolution in Corporate Culture, Berlin/New York: Springer.

Weber, Max (1976), Wirtschaft und Gesellschaft, Tübingen: J.C.B. Mohr.

Weick, Karl E. (1976), Educational Organizations as Loosely Coupled Systems, in: Administrative Science Quarterly 21, 1–19.

Weick, Karl E. (1979), The Social Psychology of Organizing, 2. ed., Reading, MA: Addison-Wesley.

White, Harrison C./Eccles, Robert G. (1986), Control via Concentration, in: Sociological Forum 1, 131–157.

Wildemann, Horst (1994), Die modulare Fabrik, 4. ed., München: TCW.

Williamson, Oliver E. (1975), Markets and Hierarchies, New York: Free Press.

Williamson, Oliver E. (1980), The Organization of Work: A Comparative Institutional Assessment, in: Journal of Economic Behavior and Organization 1, 5–38.

Willke, Helmut (1989a), Systemtheorie entwickelter Gesellschaften: Dynamik und Riskanz moderner Selbstorganisation, Weinheim/München: Juventa.

Willke, Helmut (1989b), Controlling als Kontextsteuerung. Zum Problem dezentralen Entscheidens in vernetzten Organisationen, in: Rolf Eschenbach (ed.), Supercontrolling: Vernetzt denken, zielgerichtet entscheiden, Wien: Service Fachverlag, 63–93.

Womack, James P./Jones, Daniel T./Roos, Daniel (1991), The Machine That Changed the World: The Story of Lean Production, New York: HarperCollins.

Zarifian, Philippe (1990), La nouvelle productivité, Paris: L'Harmattan.